Simply NAPKINS

No matter what your time, budget, or décor limitations,

there's space in your life for these little squares of accessible elegance.

Gail Brown and Mary Mulari

Published by

krause publications
An F&W Publications Company

700 East State Street • Iola, WI 54990-0001
715-445-2214 • 888-457-2873
www.krause.com

Library of Congress Catalog Number: 2003108201

ISBN: 0-87349-583-7

Printed in the United States of America

Photographs by Dustin Penman (portraitexpressions.com), taken at Aberdeen Mansion Bed & Breakfast (aberdeenmansionbb.com) in Aberdeen, Washington

The following company or product names appear in this book:
505®, Amazing Designs, Aqua Magic, Aquafilm, Babylock USA, Bernina, Brother International, Cactus Punch, Clover Bias Tape Maker, Clover Border Bias, Clover Fusible Web, Clover Fusible Tape Maker, Clover Mini Iron®, Clover Quick Bias, Concord House, Covington, Criswell Embroidery and Design, Dakota Collectibles, Dan River®, Deco Wrap™ No-Sew Neck Roll, DMC, Dreft®, Elna USA, Embroidery Arts, Fabric Traditions®, Finishing Touch Rayon Thread, Finishing Touch Ultra Tear-Away, FrayBlock™, FreeSpirit Fabrics Studio Collection, Ghee's Floral Dimensions, Hoffman California International Fabrics, Home-Sew, Husqvarna Viking, Hydro-Stick, Isacord, Ivory®, Janome, Jumbo Rick Rack from Wrights®, Lenox® Maywood™, Madeira Rayon Thread, Marcus Brothers Textiles, Michael Miller Fabrics, Nancy's Notions®, OESD Badgemaster, OESD Ultra Clean and Tear, Offray, Oklahoma Embroidery Supply (OESD), OxyClean®, P & B Textiles, PBS, Pellon® Stitch 'N Tear Lite, Pellon® Tear-N-Wash™, Pellon Wonder Under®, Perfect Sew™ Liquid Stabilizer, Pfaff American Sales Corp., Prym-Dritz®, Purrfection Artistic Wearables, Quilting Treasures™ by Cranston™, Radial Rule™, ReVisions, RJR Fashion Fabrics®, Robison-Anton, Sensuede™, Sewing with Nancy®, Singer, Springs Fabrics, Springs' Quilters™ Only® Fabrics, Steam-A-Seam®, Success® Acrylic Serging Yarn, Sulky KK2000®, Sulky® Rayon Thread, Sulky® Super Solvy™, Sulky® Tear-Easy™, Therm O Web HeatnBond® Lite™, Therm O Web HeatnBond® Ultra Hold, Thimbleberries®, Timeless Treasures, Ultrasuede®, Vermillion Stitchery, Viking, Viking Fuse 'n Tear, VIP by Cranston™, Washable Quick Fuse™ Inkjet Fabric from June Tailor, Woolly Nylon, Wonder Under®, Wright's® Double-Fold Bias Tape, Wright's® Extra Wide Bias Tape

Dedication

In celebration of my adopted hometown, Hoquiam, Washington
— and the proud resilience of my Grays Harbor neighbors.

— Gail Brown

For Diana Langlee, my friend and now my stepsister,
who has used and enjoyed all the napkins I've made for her.

— Mary Mulari

Table of Contents

Introduction: *Why Napkins (and This Book)?*   **6**

Chapter 1: *Fast, Fabulous Folds*   **7**
24 Featured Folds 8
Holiday Folds: Tabletop Trees 20
Rings: Ease, Elegance... Extraordinary! 21

Chapter 2: *Ready-Made Upgrades*   **31**
Gorgeous Garnishes: Stamping 32
Mary's Simple Stenciling – With Style . .34
Silk Floral Accents 36
Corner Danglers & Dazzlers 38
Custom Color Copier Creations 39

Chapter 3: *No-Sew and Low-Sew Napkins*   **41**
Fantastically Fast-Fused Edges 42
Two Seams: Simple Self-Lining 44
Terrific Topstitched Tubes 46
Fast-Framed Finish 48
Fail-Proof Fused and Stitched Binding 50

Chapter 4: *Machine-Sewn in Minutes*   **53**
A Quick Classic: Lined & Reversible . . .54
Pretty Hems, Painless Miters 56
Narrow, Nice & Simple:
    Twice-Turned Hems 58
Double-Needle Delights 60
Beautiful Borders 62
Clever Corded Wonder 64

Chapter 5: *Quilt Lovers' Napkins* 67

Fat Quarter Collection: Bias-Taped Borders 68
Foundation Strips, Fast 70
Quick "Snowball" Corners 72
Four-Way Diagonal Napkins 74
More Fat Quarter Bounty: Bias Borders 76

Chapter 6: *Serged Napkins*
**   *As Never Before* 79**

Serged Standby: Turn & Topstitch 80
Quintessentially Napkins: Narrow-Rolled Edges . .82
Wrapped-Edge Finish 84
Sleek Serged Banding 86

Chapter 7: *Machine Embroidery Showcase* 89

Chapter 8: *Napkins As Gifts and Décor* 97

As Seasonal Gift Sets 98
    As Gift Wrap or Presentations 99
    As Basket Fillers, Liners & Accents 100
    As Special Occasion Settings 101
    As Other Table Linens 102
    As Coasters, Cozies & Covers 103
    As Pillows, Bolsters, Slipcovers & Table Toppers .104
    As Décor 106
    As Covers, Fillers & Accents 107
    As Aprons 108
    As Totes 110

Chapter 9: *Time- and Money-Saving Guide*   111

Napkin Fabrics: Key Questions & Sources 112
User-Friendly Folding Tips 113
Reviving Vintage Linens 114
Serging: Gail's Tried & True Tips 115
Cutting Out: Our Timesaving Template
    System .116
Bias Strips: Yardages & How-Tos 118

Hemstitching: A Classic Returns . .120
Easiest Machine Embroidery
    Strategies 121
Mary's Monograms 122
Mary's Appliqués: Tips & Designs . .124
Ready Reference: Table Setting
    Templates 125

About the Authors   126
Sources for Napkin Making (and Napkins)   127
Index   128

Introduction

Why Napkins (and This Book)?

Simply put, we love napkins and think you will, too — for their beauty, practicality, affordability, recyclability, and fun. No matter what your time, budget, or décor limitations, there's space in your life for these little squares of accessible elegance. Experience has taught us that napkins somehow improve our cooking too; we know, unequivocally, that meals always taste better when served with cloth napkins.

We set out to answer the obvious questions about napkins: Where can I find fast and easy ways to fold napkins? What can I do to upgrade or embellish ho-hum ready-mades? How can I make my own napkins — whether or not I know how to sew? Then we went a few steps further into our love affair with napkins and asked: How can I use napkins as gifts, furnishings, and fashions? (Gail may have carried this too far: She coordinated dog and décor, dressing her black Labrador, Gunnar, in a napkin bandana — see page 101.)

Every project was designed to fit your busy lifestyle. Featured folds don't require extra pressing, starching, or more than a few simple steps. The materials we used are not exotic — most are readily available at local variety and fabric stores, and if not, through reliable mail order sources. (We both live in lovely little towns with limited retail outlets. What you see in this book is from Aurora, Minnesota, and Hoquiam, Washington, population 1,800 and 9,000, respectively.)

If any fold, finish, or flourish puzzles you, please write. Our Web sites include bonus book updates and links to our e-mail addresses, and we hope you will visit often (www.marymulari.com and www.gailbrown.com). Also, watch for Mary and host Nancy Zieman on *Sewing with Nancy* (PBS) and the video version of *Simply Napkins* (available from Nancy's Notions, www.nancysnotions.com). You might also find Mary at consumer sewing shows, machine dealer conventions, and retail stores, sharing her unique brand of lively how-tos — and humor. For now, Gail is taking a break from TV and public appearances but will continue to write and answer your mail.

Enjoy this book — and napkins.

Mary Mulari

Gail Brown

Chapter 1
Fast, Fabulous Folds

Fabric: "Red on Red! Kiss the Cook" from Dan River.

You may never have the time or inclination to make napkins. But anyone, any age, nearly anywhere, can enjoy napkin folding. The 27 folds featured in this chapter are intentionally easy, requiring only a few steps and no additional pressing or starching.

Frappucino

- Best for squares 15" to 20" (20" size is shown here and on page 33).
- Cut ribbon lengths 24" to 27".
- Saves space on a crowded table.
- Shows off corner detail or border.
- Test: Can the napkin stand in the glass?

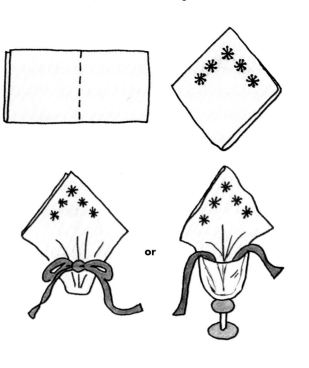

or

Soft Crown

- Best for squares 15" to 20" (20" size is shown here and on page 35).
- Dramatically displays napkin, ring, and plate.
- Shows off corner detail or border.
- Vary with other ring styles (see pages 21 to 30).

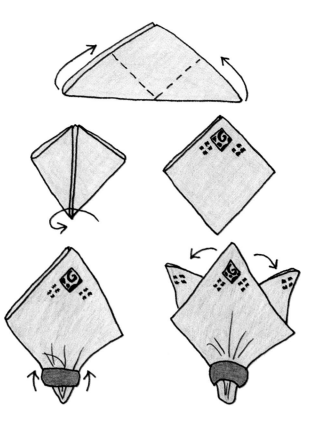

Ascot

- Best for squares 15" to 22" (22" size is shown here and on page 37).
- Place on or next to plate.
- Shows off corner detail or border.
- Vary with a tie or ring (see Tied Ascot, pages 19 and 85).

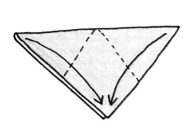

Flame

- Best for squares 15" to 20" (18" size is shown here and on page 43).
- Add weight and contrast with a second napkin (the lighter-color print).
- Use firm, tightly woven fabrics.
- Test: Can the ring hold the napkin upright?

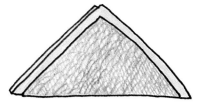

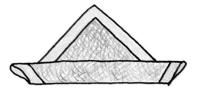

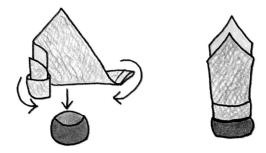

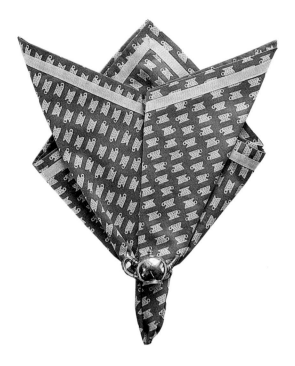

Wings

- Best for squares 18" to 22" (18" size is shown here and on page 45).
- Saves space on a crowded table.
- Shows off corner detail or border.
- Substitute a ring for the glass.
- Test: Can the napkin stand in the glass?

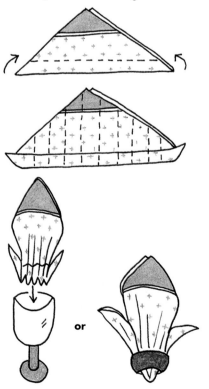

Flair

- Best for squares 15" to 20" (18" size is shown here and on page 47).
- With a ring, place on the plate; without a ring, place under the plate.
- Shows off border trim.
- Starch and press for sharper creases.
- Vary by rolling the corners (see Rolled Flair, page 13).

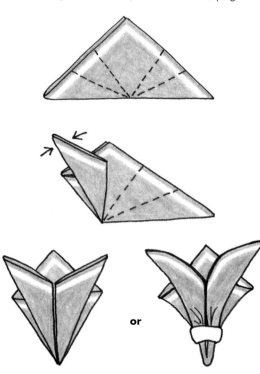

Fabric Fan

- Best for squares 15" to 22" (20" size is shown here, on the cover, and on page 49).
- Shows off border trim.
- Line with a contrasting color napkin (see Bordered Fan, pages 13 and 61).
- Move the ring to resize the fan depth.

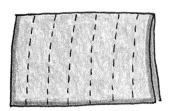

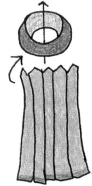

or

Bouquet

- Best for squares 15" to 20" (15" size is shown here and on page 51).
- Maximizes size with asymmetrical fold.
- Hides wrinkles and stains in gathers.
- Move the ring to resize the bouquet.
- Vary with other ring styles.

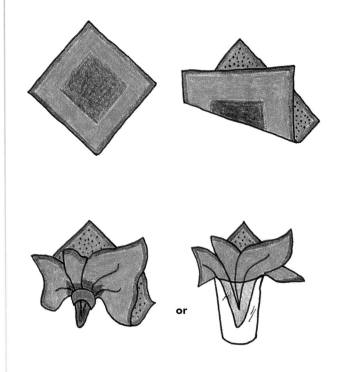

or

Peaks Peeking

- Best for squares 18" to 22" with contrasting lining (20" size is shown here and on page 55).
- Fold slightly askew to expose lining.
- With a ring, place on the plate; without a ring, place under the plate.
- Starch and press for sharper creases.
- Vary with other ring styles (see pages 21 to 30).

Banana Peel

- Best for squares 18" to 22" (19" size is shown here and on page 57).
- Place on a plate or around a glass.
- Shows off stripes.
- For a less relaxed look, starch and press sharper creases.

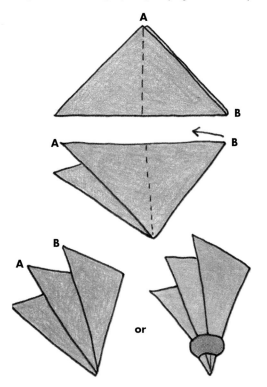

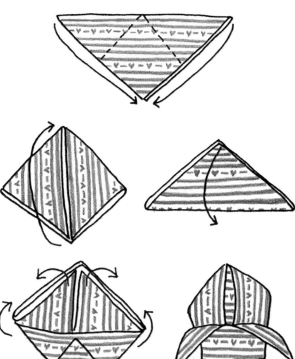

Rolled Flair

- Best for squares 15" to 20" (19" size is shown here and on page 59).
- Fold with or without a ring.
- Use a napkin with a flexible edge that will roll.
- Vary by not rolling the corners (see Flair, page 10).

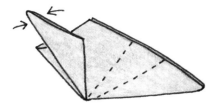

Bordered Fan

- Best for squares 15" to 20" (20" size is shown here and on page 61).
- Shows off the border stitching or trim.
- Fold together with a contrasting color "lining" to add weight and color contrast, while hiding the wrong sides.
- Move the ring to resize the fan depth.

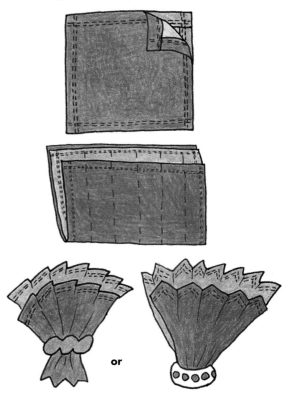

or

Pocket

- Best for squares 15" to 22" (20" size is shown here and on page 63).
- Place on or next to the plate.
- Shows off the corner detail or border.
- Vary with a tie or ring.

Early American

- Best for squares 18" to 22" (21" size is shown here and on page 65).
- Place on, next to, or above the plate.
- Use a napkin with a flat edge that's not bulky.
- For a crisper look, starch and press sharper creases.

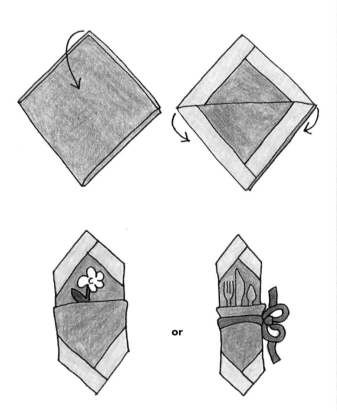

or

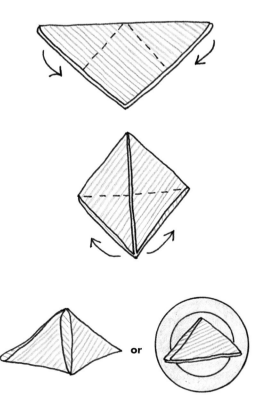

or

Quilters' Heart

- Best for rectangles (17" x 19" size is shown here and on page 69). The border is the 17" side.
- Shows off the border and rectangular shape.
- Starch and press for sharper creases.
- Vary with other ring styles (see pages 21 to 30) or by folding the point under.

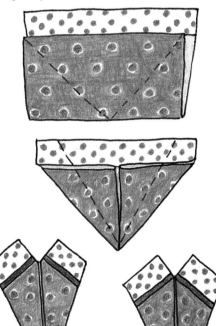

or

Simple Pleat

- Best for squares 15" to 22" (20" size is shown here and on page 71).
- Place on or next to the plate.
- Roll and tie to create a utensil pocket.
- Vary with a ring; move the ring to restyle the fold.

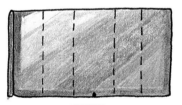

or

fold in half again

Candle in a Cup

- Best for squares 18" to 22" (18" size is shown here and on page 73).
- Saves space on a crowded table.
- Shows off the corner detail or border.
- Substitute a ring for the glass.
- Test: Can the napkin stand in the glass?

Trumpet Garden

- Best for squares 15" to 22" (19" size is shown here and on page 75).
- Place on or next to the plate.
- Shows off the pieced seaming and contrasting colors.
- Vary with other ring styles (see pages 21 to 30).

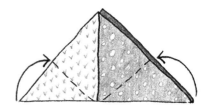

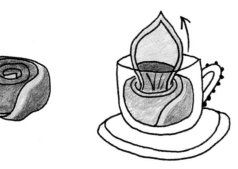

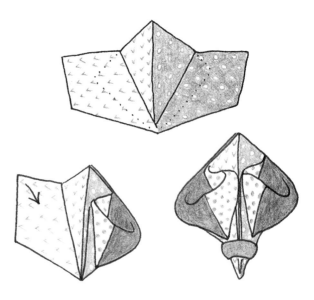

Forget-Me-Knot

- Best for rectangles or squares 17" to 22" (17" size is shown here and on page 77).
- Knot loosely, so the napkin can be easily opened.
- Thread favors or utensils through the knot.
- Knot a set for a buffet or gift basket.

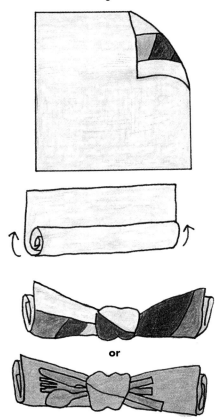

or

Roll Call

- Best for squares or rectangles, any size (17" banner shape is shown here and on page 78).
- Place on or next to the plate.
- Shows off the border trim.
- Vary with other ring styles (see pages 21 to 30).

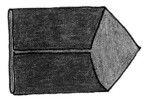

or

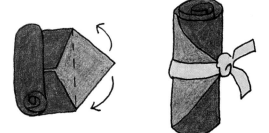

Peacock

- Best for squares 18" to 22" (18" size is shown here and on page 81).
- Shows off the corner detail or border.
- Saves space on a crowded table.
- Starch and press for more precise pleats.

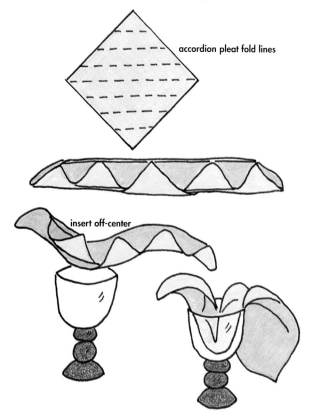

accordion pleat fold lines

insert off-center

Potted Plant

- Suitable for circles 15" to 22" (17" size, including trim, is shown here and on page 83).
- Maximizes size with the layered fold.
- Hides wrinkles and stains in the gathers.
- Use other "pots" such as a jean pocket (page 21) or cones (page 27).

Tied Ascot

- Best for squares 15" to 22" (18" size is shown here and on page 85).
- Place on or next to the plate.
- Shows off the corner detail or border.
- Vary by not tying (see Ascot, pages 9 and 37).

Victory

- Best for squares 18" to 22" (18" size is shown here and on page 87).
- Saves space on a crowded table.
- Shows off the binding or decorative stitching.
- Can be placed in a glass or ring.
- Vary by not rolling the last 4" to 5".

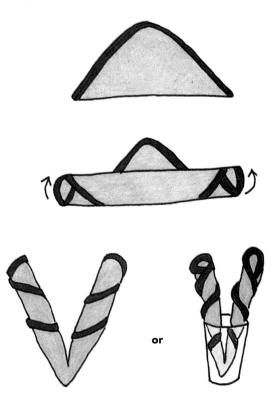

or

Holiday Folds: Tabletop Trees

Rain Forest Fir

20"-22" napkin: quarter fold as in first illustration
smaller napkin: single layer (as in photo)

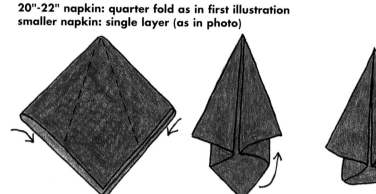

Fabric: "Fireside Holiday" from Fabric Traditions. Binding: Clover Border Bias.

Quinault Tall

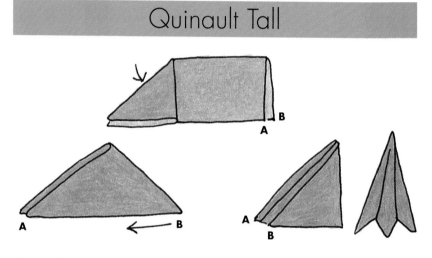

Fabric: "Fireside Holiday" from Fabric Traditions.

Grays Harbor Garland

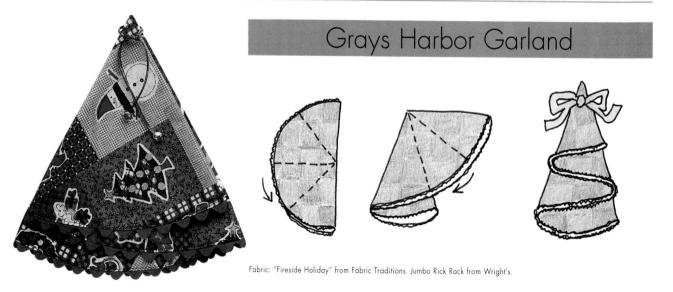

Fabric: "Fireside Holiday" from Fabric Traditions. Jumbo Rick Rack from Wright's.

Rings: Ease, Elegance... Extraordinary!

Pull a corner or the center of the napkin through a cup handle. For the fullest fold, see Bouquet on page 11.

Wind and twist the stem around three fingers or an empty gift-wrap tube. With wire cutters or crummy scissors, cut off the excess stem.

Fabric: "Rose Pavilion" from VIP by Cranston.

Fabric: "Vintage Chic" from Dan River.

Cup Handle

"Silk" Flower

Wooden Curtain Ring

Jean Pocket

Use pliers to screw on the eyelet from a 2" ring. Optional: Stain or paint the unfinished rings.

Trim away the jean fabric close to the pocket edges; finish the edges with sealant such as FrayBlock. Mix pocket styles for a fun table setting.

Fabric: "Thimbleberries Sunshine & Shadows" from RJR Fashion Fabrics.

Fabric: "Bandana Classics" from VIP by Cranston.

Rings That Tie

Gather a handful of raffia strands and tie them around a napkin. For a simple knot, use a 10" length, for a bow tie, use 15". Inexpensive and disposable.

Fabric: "A Joyful Christmas" from Marcus Brothers Textiles.

Pull the napkin through the tassel loop, as shown, or use "chair ties" with tassels on both ends of an 18" satin cord – perfect for napkin tying (see pages 17 and 78).

Fabric: "Bali Batiks" from Hoffman California International Fabrics.

Raffia Ties

Tassels

Mini-Mitten

Embroidered Ribbon

Simply insert the center of the napkin into a mini-mitten. Or hand stitch mini-mittens to a 15" strand of yarn or ribbon and wrap it around the napkin.

Fabric: Mary Mulari's "Knittin' Mittens" from Marcus Brothers Textiles.

Cut 18" lengths of ribbon and embroider them with your sewing machine. Place the ribbon over two layers of water-soluble stabilizer and stitch either the entire length or just the ends.

Fabric: "Blue Solstice" from P & B Textiles. Wire-edged ribbon from Offray.

Rings That Are Gifts

Tie on a tag with the guest's name and remind your guests that the cookie cutters are a gift. Stars, trees, and leaf shapes work well.

Fabric: "Bookbinders" by Timeless Treasures.

Stretchy ponytail holders double perfectly as pretty, practical party favors. To hold the gathers more securely, first place a covered hair band on the napkin and cover it with the pretty ponytail holder.

Fabric: "Bird Tree" by Springs' Quilters Only Fabrics.

Cookie Cutters

Ponytail Holders

Key Rings

Children's Bracelets

Go on a treasure hunt at sporting goods, hardware, or drug stores for creative napkin ring possibilities. Anything roundish, 2" to 3" in diameter, works well.

Fabric: "Holiday Spirit" from Springs Fabrics.

Go for funky and bright, stretchy and sturdy. Or, if using a nonstretch solid, find something no more than 3" in diameter.

Fabric: "Pennsylvania Plain & Fancy" from P & B Textiles.

Ring in the Holidays

Pin or glue sewn or purchased appliqués on a ready-made ring. Here a machine-embroidered poinsettia from Cactus Punch's "Ghee's Floral Dimensions" complements the holiday-themed fabric.

Fabric: "Holiday Spirit" from Springs Fabrics.

Brass horns are easy to find, afford, and use. For extra color and texture, loop on a tassel.

Fabric: "Holiday Spirit" from Springs Fabrics.

Dimensionals

Ornaments

Mini-Wreaths

Jingle Bell Ties!

Try festive, economical mini-wreaths – either a candle ring, as shown, or a grapevine or ornament. You will find an endless variety in craft stores.

Fabric: Mary Mulari's "A Joyful Christmas" from Marcus Brothers Textiles.

Cut a 15" length of ¼" satin cord. Tape, snip, and knot the ends to prevent raveling. Then pry open ½" to ¾" jingle bells, insert the cord, and close the opening with needlenose pliers.

Fabric: "Contemporary Christmas" from Concord House.

Fabric Rosette Rings

Create rosette rings to complement table linens, place settings, a party theme, or a special occasion. These are ideal as bouquet accents too.

Fabric: "Stripes Galore" from FreeSpirit Fabrics.

place on bias fold

Rosette Pattern

lengthwise or crosswise grain

Six Easy Steps

1. Trace the pattern on this page.

2. Place the straight edge along the bias fold of a piece of fabric. Cut one for each rosette.

3. With a long machine stitch, sew the wavy edges together. Secure the tails of the threads on one end and carefully pull from the other end to gather the threads. A rosette shape will form.

4. With the gathering thread tails, sew into one end of the fabric strip to secure the stitches. Then roll the strip to form a rosette shape. Make a few more stitches through all the layers to hold the rosette together.

5. Cut the leaf shape from felt, synthetic suede, or other nonfraying fabric. Or cut the leaf from fabric, seam with ¼" seam allowances, and turn right side out.

leaf with tuck folded to center

6. Hand stitch the leaf to the underside of the rosette. Then hand stitch the flower to a stretchy ponytail holder.

fold a tuck here

Leaf Pattern

cut both patterns to size

Fabric: "Sweetbriar" from Marcus Brothers Textiles.

Quick! Paper Ring Creations

Try using these quick creations as name cards. You can hand letter, type, or print the guests' names on the rings. For a lively dinner party, write clever quotes or conversation starters. Or place a photo in the frame motif, rather than a name.

Three Easy Steps

1. Photocopy or trace the patterns on this page. No enlargement is necessary.
2. Cut the rings out of heavy paper, card stock, or nonfraying fabrics such as oilcloth, felt, Ultrasuede, or Sensuede.
3. Interlock the ends, as shown.

Paper too flimsy? If your paper seems too thin to hold up, fuse two layers together, using paper-backed fusible web. Gail also favors laminating paper rings, doubling their durability and ease of cutting. For an interesting variation, use fabric as the second layer, fusing it to the paper before cutting out the pattern.

fold rings together

Nifty Napkin Cones

Transform any setting with these dramatic, easy-to-make napkin cones. Sensuede, Ultrasuede, felt, oilcloth, and crisp lace all work well. Or use a vintage handkerchief or the corner of a napkin – anything that will wrap to form a cone. Just pull the center of the napkin into the cone. Then get ready for lots of compliments.

Embroidery: Design from BabyLock Ellagéo 3 machine on ready-made napkin.

Three Easy Steps

1. Photocopy the pattern from this page at 125%.

2. Cut it out from fabric. If you are using fabric that frays, hem the top and corner edges by turning them under ¼" and machine stitching, or fuse the edges in place using ½" wide fusible web strips (see Featured Materials, page 42).

3. Machine stitch the seam using a ¼" allowance. If you are using paper, lap the paper over and glue or staple.

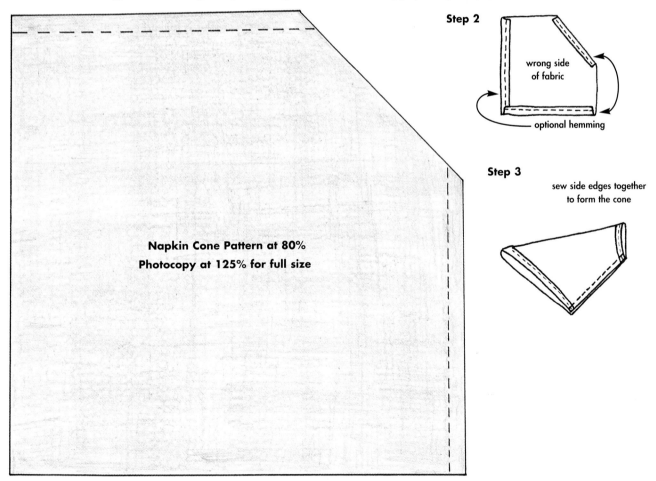

Napkin Cone Pattern at 80%
Photocopy at 125% for full size

Step 2

wrong side of fabric

optional hemming

Step 3

sew side edges together to form the cone

No-Sew Ring Innovations

If you can cut and press, you can make these rings. They store conveniently flat, then interlock to form a ring shape.

Interlocking Rings

Four Easy Steps

1. Photocopy the pattern or shape of your choice from this page at 125%.

2. Using paper-backed fusible web, fuse together two layers of non-fraying fabric (Ultrasuede, Sensuede, felt, vinyl, or oilcloth). Use a press cloth to protect any heat-sensitive fabrics during fusing.

3. From the fused fabric, cut out the ring(s).

4. Cut along the lines indicated to create the interlocking, as shown.

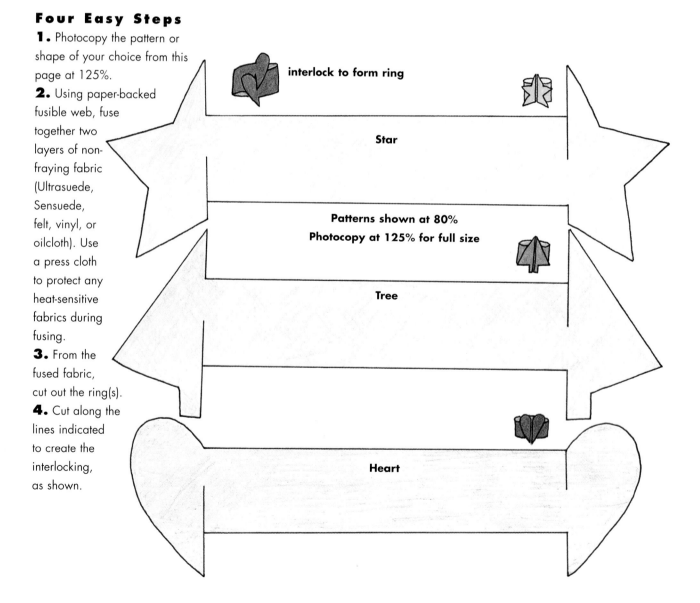

interlock to form ring

Star

Patterns shown at 80%
Photocopy at 125% for full size

Tree

Heart

leaf
bow tie

cut line C

Nonfraying fabrics such as felt, Sensuede, Ultrasuede, vinyl, or oilcloth make this lovely ring fast and fun.

Fabric: Leather-like snakeskin vinyl tied around ready-made napkin.

Bow Tie Rings

Six Easy Steps

Optional: For additional stability, fuse nonwoven interfacing to the wrong side of the fabric.

1. Photocopy or trace the pattern from this page. No enlargement is necessary.

2. From nonfraying fabric, trace and cut out the ring(s).

3. On a cutting board, cut the three lines with a buttonhole cutter or sharp utility knife.

4. Pull the end with the two cut lines A and B through cut line C.

5. Pull the other end through the two cut lines A and B. Adjust the two ends so they are even, as shown in the photo.

6. For a bow tie look, trim to square off the leaves, as shown.

bow tie ring

cut line B

cut line A

bow tie

leaf

Gail's Garland Twist

There's so much wired garland in Gail's attic that Mary suspects some sort of spontaneous reproduction. Ring making will shrink the inventory overload, and the results are dazzling.

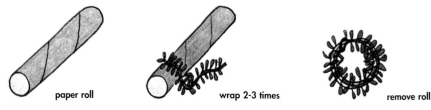

paper roll   wrap 2-3 times   remove roll

Ready-made napkin.

Chainstitched Cord or Trim

Transform cord or trim into an elegant textured ring. As an added embellishment, accent the cord with a tassel.

Three Easy Steps

1. Cut a 30" length of a ½" satin cord. Tape both ends.

2. Chainstitch six or seven knots and pull the tail through the last loop.

3. Weave the cord tails back through the first and last loops to form a ring. Weave the tails back into the chain to secure them.

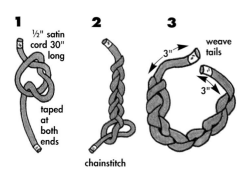

1 ½" satin cord 30" long / taped at both ends

2 chainstitch

3 weave tails / 3" / 3"

Satin cord: Prym-Dritz on ready-made napkin.

Fabric-Covered Paper Roll

These bargain rings still make sense, taking beautiful advantage of coordinating fabric borders and stripes.

Three Easy Steps

1. Cut a paper roll open. Cut pieces of fabric and fusible web slightly larger than the paper roll dimensions.

2. Fuse the wrong side of the fabric to the flattened roll. Turn and fuse the fabric edges over the roll edges, on all but one short end.

3. Overlap the short ends to reassemble the roll and carefully fuse or staple the paper roll back together, without crushing the roll.

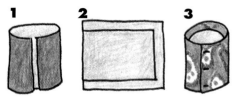

1   **2**   **3**

Fabric: "Tossed Bandana Paisley" by Springs Fabrics.

Chapter 2
Ready-Made Upgrades

Problem: *Ho-hum napkins.* **Solution:** *Surface excitement – stamping, stenciling, photo transfer, appliqués, and pockets, all featured in this chapter. Makeover candidates are waiting in your linen drawers and on clearance sale tables.*

Gorgeous Garnishes: Stamping

Rubber stamps are everywhere, and stamping is a fast, fun way to upgrade ready-made napkins. Stage a stamping party – guests young and old will be fascinated by this hands-on craft and their personalized designs.

Four Easy Steps

1. Work on a hard surface protected with paper. Follow the instructions for your paint. Practice techniques on paper and fabric scraps before stamping on the napkins.

Plan the layout on the napkin by cutting stamped images out of paper and positioning them in a pleasing arrangement. Remove the paper images one at a time just before stamping on the fabric. The images can be centered on a corner and/or edge, or sprinkled around the surface. (A)

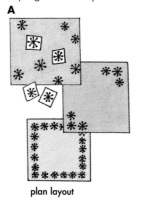

A

plan layout

2. Spread fabric paint on a blank stamp pad or a dampened stack of felt. Lightly tap the stamp on the pad. Press the stamp down evenly on the paint pad. Check to see that all the areas of the stamp are covered with paint before stamping on the fabric.

3. Carefully lift and remove the stamp and press it on the napkin. (B) Tap the stamp on the inkpad again and continue stamping.

Note: *Clean stamps immediately after use. Premoistened wipes work well as interim cleaners, but before storage, clean the stamp with a soft toothbrush and mild dishwashing detergent.*

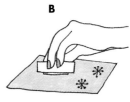

B

stamp on napkin

4. Allow the stamped images to dry completely, then heat set them with a dry iron. To prevent bleeding, peeling, or fading, allow the stamped napkins to cure 24 to 48 hours before using or laundering them.

Featured Materials

- *Stamps.* Stamps with a detailed image work best on smooth-surfaced fabrics; solid image stamps are a better choice for coarse fabrics.
- *Laundered napkins.* Machine washing and drying removes the sizing, ensuring that the stamp paint will adhere and remain vibrant through future laundering.
- *Fabric paint.* Find fabric paint at craft, fabric, and variety stores. Or use a pre-inked fabric paint pad.
- *Blank ink pad.* If you don't have a stamp pad, stack three layers of felt and dampen with water sprayed from a bottle.
- *Butcher or freezer paper* for protecting the table surface and for practice stamping.

Frappucino

Find step-by-step folding instructions on page 8.

Rubber stamp: "Snowflakes" from Purrfection Artistic Wearables on ready-made napkin.

Sometimes a strategically chosen fold can disguise minor goof-ups. Mary, an ambitious newcomer to stamping, positioned the corner with her best attempt to be the most exposed. Gail hails from the espresso-loving Pacific Northwest, and couldn't resist calling the drink-shaped fold Frappucino.

Mary's Simple Stenciling – With Style

Just about anyone can stencil successfully – and stylishly. And there's not a handier, more portable palette than napkins. Get creative stenciling the corners, borders, or the entire square.

Four Easy Steps

1. Work on a hard surface protected with paper. Pour a dab of paint on a foam plate. Dip the applicator into the paint, then rub off most of the paint on an empty area of the plate. Use very little paint on the applicator to avoid forming a stiff stencil on the fabric. Practice stenciling on paper and scrap fabric. Lightly tap the applicator over the open areas of the stencil. Try applying more paint to the outer outline of the stencil motif. With practice, it's easy to create the stenciled look you want. (A)

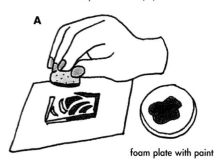

foam plate with paint

2. Plan the layout on the napkin by cutting stenciled images out of paper and positioning them in a pleasing arrangement. Remove the paper images one-by-one just before stenciling on the fabric. (B)

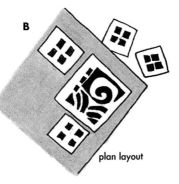

plan layout

3. After completing the paint application, lift the stencil off the napkin. Handle the stencil with care, cleaning your fingers as you work. Before use or laundering, dry or heat set, following the fabric paint label instructions. Allow the stenciled napkin to dry for at least 24 hours.

4. If the stencil is made of plastic or acetate, clean it by soaking it in warm water. Wipe off any remaining paint residue with rubbing alcohol. Store dry, clean stencils in file folders, keeping them flat and protected for future use.

Featured Materials

- *Precut stencil.* Any precut stencil that works well in a corner or along an edge.
- *Laundered napkins.* Machine wash and dry to remove the sizing, ensuring that the stencil paint will adhere and remain vibrant through future laundering.
- *Fabric paint.* Find at craft, fabric, and variety stores.
- *Paint applicator.* Sponge, dense foam rubber, or stencil brush.
- *Foam plate* or any disposable, cleanable surface for holding the paint.
- *Butcher or freezer paper* for protecting the table surface and testing.

Soft Crown

Find step-by-step folding instructions on page 8.

Stencil: ReVisions' "Off the Wall" by Diane Ericson on ready-made napkin.

Mary's stencil choice looks stunning with Gail's hand-painted Italian plate, or consider duplicating your own dinnerware motifs. Cut the stencils from acetate sheets or clear plastic report covers.

Silk Floral Accents

Using dinnerware motifs as the design inspiration, you can accent napkins with matching silk flowers. Shop for artificial flowers with a dish – or photo – in hand. Mary used a color snapshot, sent across the country by e-mail, when selecting flowers to coordinate with Gail's vintage china pattern.

Four Easy Steps

1. Trim the petals and leaves from the stems. Cut off the stem right below the flower and slide off the flower layers. Peel the plastic veins off the back side of the leaves. Using a press cloth, press the flower and leaf layers flat. (A)

A

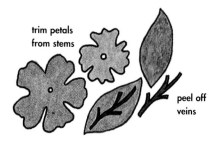

trim petals from stems

peel off veins

2. Trace around the flower and leaf shapes on the paper side of the fusible web. Cut out the shapes, trimming them slightly smaller than the tracings. Fuse the paper shapes to the wrong sides of the flowers and the leaves. Peel off the paper. (B)

B

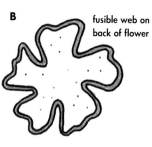

fusible web on back of flower

3. Position the flowers and leaves on the napkin, following the dinnerware pattern or your own design. Fuse the shapes to the napkins. (C)

Optional: Cover the small hole in the center of the flower with a tiny piece cut from an extra petal, or with a button.

4. Launder these decorated napkins in a mesh bag to protect the floral decorations. Press the napkins and the floral decorations after laundering.

C

napkin accents

Variations

Embellish a table runner to match. (D) The napkins and table runner shown on page 37 were recycled from sections of an old tablecloth from Mary's collection; the fused-on flowers camouflage discolorations.

D

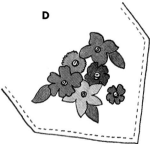

runner accents

Featured Materials

- *Silk flowers and leaves.* Look for lightweight, silk-like petals and leaves. The stems will be trimmed off.
- *Ready-made napkins.* No need to pre-launder.
- *Paper-backed fusible web.* ¼ yard heavy-duty or no-sew. Brands to look for include Wonder Under Heavy Duty or Therm O Web HeatnBond Ultra Hold Iron-On Adhesive. Follow the manufacturer's instructions when fusing.
- *Wire cutters or crummy utility scissor* for trimming the artificial flowers.
- *Press cloth* or sheet for protecting the petals and leaves when pressing.

Ascot

Find step-by-step folding instructions on page 9.

Mary's initial intention was to more closely match the china pattern shown here. Still, her generic dimensional appliqués were charming and blended beautifully with Gail's heirlooms. When Mary stitched button centers on the blossoms, we agreed that the extra touches of color and texture were just right.

Tassel: Prym-Dritz on ready-made napkin.

Corner Danglers & Dazzlers

Banish dull corners! Transform ordinary napkins into extraordinary ones by simply adding tassels or beads. Corner enhancements make sense, too, because they don't detract from the practical purpose of napkins: wiping faces and hands.

Easy Steps

• **Tassels**. Hand sew two small buttons on the corner of the napkin. Place the buttons a short distance apart so the loop of the tassel can wrap around them in a figure-eight. Then you can easily remove the tassels before washing the napkins. (A)

• **Beads**. Thread the needle with a double strand of all-purpose thread. To prevent the beads from slipping off, tie two knots in the thread ends. Insert the threaded needle into the corner hem, gently tugging on the strands to make sure the knot will hold. Anchor with two small hidden stitches. Slide the beads through the needle, ending with a small bead. Pull the thread through and around the final bead, then back up through the other beads to the corner of the napkin. Anchor the thread again, knot, and hide the thread tails in the hem. To protect the beads, launder the napkins by machine in a mesh bag or by hand. (B)

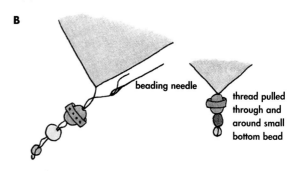

Featured Materials

• *Beads*. Look for the types illustrated here in bead, craft, fabric, and variety stores.
• *Tassels*. Any small tassel works well.
• *Ready-made or custom-made napkins*. No need to pre-launder.
• *Needles*. Hand sewing needles for tassels, a beading needle (or any narrow and long enough) for beads.
• *Small buttons*. Two for each tassel corner.

Custom Color Copier Creations

It's this easy: Use a color inkjet copier or printer to transfer images onto special fusible fabric. Then fuse your newly printed fabric to napkins as appliqués and trim.

Appliqué: Washable Quick Fuse Inkjet Fabric Sheets by June Tailor on ready-made napkin.

Three Easy Steps

1. Transfer the image to the fabric sheet. For the most economical use of the sheets, plan to copy or print several images to fit in the 8½" x 11" size. Place the images on the glass bed of a copier and do a test using standard paper. If you are using a printer, scan the images and test-print on standard printer paper. Load the fabric transfer sheet(s) into the copier or printer so that it prints on the fabric side. Allow the ink to dry. (A)

A

print images on fabric sheet

2. Cut out, fuse, and stitch the images to the napkin. Cut out the printed images and thoroughly fuse them to the napkin using medium heat (no steam) for five seconds. Sew around the edges with a medium-length, medium-width zigzag or decorative stitch to permanently secure. (B)

B

3. Launder the finished napkin following package instructions. Skip the detergent — instead use a small amount of all-color liquid bleach and liquid fabric softener with cold water. If machine washing, use the gentle cycle. You can also hand wash. Lay the napkins flat to dry and press.

Featured Materials

- *Fusible inkjet transfer fabric.* Washable Quick Fuse Inkjet Fabric Sheets from June Tailor are available in white and ivory from fabric and craft stores and by mail order.
- *Image(s) for transferring.* Photos, clip art, sheet music, magazine pages, invitations, announcements, even flowers from your backyard. Honor copyrights and inquire if uncertain.
- *Ready-made or custom-made napkins.* No need to pre-launder.

Chopsticks Pocket and Appliqués

These napkins are charming with or without chopsticks (or Chinese food).

For the pocket, cut one rectangle 2½" x 6". Cut two appliqués, one 4" x 5" and one 4" x 3". Turn under ¼" on all edges of the three rectangles and press.

Using the photograph and illustration as guides, pin and edgestitch the rectangles to the right side of the napkin, leaving one side of the pocket unstitched.

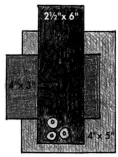

pocket and appliqué arrangement

Fabrics: "Thimbleberries Sunshine & Shadows" from RJR Fashion Fabrics on ready-made napkin.

Place Card Windows

Whether they hold a name, message, or fortune card, the vinyl windows are certain to keep the conversation – and fun – flowing.

Cut a piece of clear vinyl for the window, 1½" x 2½". Position the vinyl window on the napkin corner, either horizontally or vertically, and secure it with transparent (cloudy) tape. Edgestitch on two long sides of the vinyl. If you have a Teflon presser foot, use it to glide over the vinyl. Cut a paper card about 1" x 3". Write a message on the card and insert it in the window. Wash the finished napkin carefully, being careful to never press the vinyl.

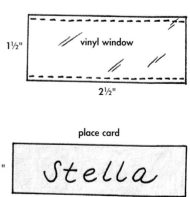

Ready-made napkin.

Chapter 3
No-Sew and Low-Sew Napkins

Perhaps you don't know how to sew. Or you can sew, but have difficulty setting aside time for it. Whatever your obstacles, the napkin projects in this chapter can help. From no-sew fusing to folded miters, the stunning results belie their modest demands on your schedule.

Fantastically Fast-Fused Edges

We confess: When in a hurry, we often fuse rather than sew napkins. Not only is this fusing technique relaxing, it's amazingly washable as well.

Four Easy Steps

1. Carefully cut out the napkin squares, using our template system (see page 116).

2. Paper-side-up, fuse the web strips to the wrong side of two opposite edges. (A) Steam-A-Seam can be finger-pressed in place but we usually fuse it so the edge is firmer for finishing. **Note:** *Before removing the paper, we recommend you barely trim the fused edges with pinking shears or a pinked- or waved-edge rotary cutter.*

3. Remove the paper from the fused web on both sides of the napkin. Finger-press the hem in half, web-to-web. The webbed edges will adhere instantly. Press to fuse in place. The finished hem will measure ¼" to ⅜" or about half the fusible web strip width. (B)

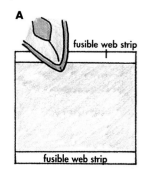

fusible web strip

fusible web strip

optional: pink or wave cut edges

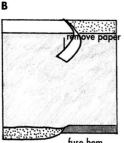

remove paper

fuse hem

4. Repeat Steps 2 and 3 for the remaining opposite sides. (C)

Washability Note: *Fused edges are seldom loosened by laundering, but if they are, re-fuse by pressing the edges again. Any stray threads can be quickly clipped too.*

Variations

Use your machine's built-in embroidery or utilitarian stitches to decorate the hemmed napkin edges. (D) Fusing stabilizes the fabric so that stitches form consistently and pucker-free.

Fusing Variation: *Mary doesn't worry about fusing web-to-web (Step 3). She generally fuses with ½" wide fusible web strip, fusing the full width of the strip (½" strip = ½ hem).*

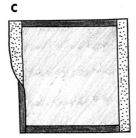

fuse remaining hems

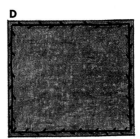

decorate hem edges

Featured Materials

- *Fabrics.* Any light- to medium-weight, tightly woven cotton, cotton blend, or other natural fiber fabric.
- *Fusible web strips (paper-backed),* ½" to ⅞" wide. You will need about 2½ yards for most napkin sizes 15" to 20" square, so a 10 yard roll will hem four napkins, a 13 yard roll will hem five napkins, and a 20 yard roll will hem about eight napkins. Brand names to look for include Steam-A-Seam (½" x 10 or 20 yard roll) and Therm O Web HeatnBond Lite (½" to ⅞" wide x 10 yard roll). *Caution:* Test fusible web strips labeled "no-sew" first – some can be too stiff and heavy for lighter weight fabrics.

Flame

Find step-by-step folding instructions on page 9.

Fabrics: "Bookbinders" from Timeless Treasures.

To add weight and color contrast, Gail made a second fused-edge napkin to use as lining. When folding the two napkins together, Mary offset the edges about ½", creating a border. Fused napkins are favorites for folds such as Flame (above and on page 9) because the firm edges will stand in an upright position.

Two Seams: Simple Self-Lining

Many terrific prints are quilt weight, which is a bit light when used as a single layer for napkins. Add weight and body with this ingenious seaming strategy.

Five Easy Steps

1. Carefully cut out the napkin squares, using our template system (see page 116). Larger squares will yield larger napkins. (A) Try to cut out true squares so the finished napkin will lie flat.

2. Fold the square in half, right sides together. Straight stitch the ends with a ½" seam allowance. (B)

3. Press the seams open and clip the allowances to minimize bulk at the corners. Refold the napkin, aligning the seamlines. To make sure the napkin will lie flat (and to compensate for off-grain fabric or out-of-square cutting), press mark the

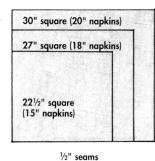

A

| 30" square (20" napkins) |
| 27" square (18" napkins) |
| 22½" square (15" napkins) |

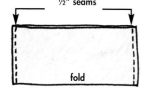

B

½" seams

fold

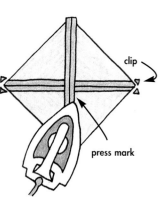

C

clip

press mark

seam allowances by first placing the napkin, seam side up, on the ironing board or surface. Then narrow or widen the seam to flatten the napkin, and press mark the seamline. (C)

4. Sew the seam, using ½" seam allowances and shortening the stitches at the ends and the opening to secure the threads. (D) Lightly press the seam open, flattening the allowances. Turn the napkin right side out.

5. Fuse or hand stitch the seam opening closed. From the unseamed side of the napkin, topstitch about 1" from the edges. (Topstitching will keep the top and "lining" layers aligned through use and laundering.)

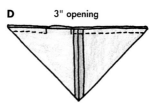

D

3" opening

Variations

Take advantage of a border print or stripe. When seamed, a border print running parallel with one edge will create corner interest, as shown in the photo on page 45. Similarly, stripes cut out parallel with an edge will seam into bias stripes on the right side of the napkin.

Featured Materials

- *Fabrics.* Any light- to medium-weight, tightly woven cotton, cotton blend, or other natural fiber fabric. Using 44"/45" fabric, 1¼ yards will yield four 15" napkins, 3 yards will yield four 18" napkins, and 3½ yards will yield four 20" napkins. For the least waste, determine the square size this way: Divide the usable width of the 44"/45" (or wider) fabric in half (usually about 22½"), yielding 15" finished napkins.

Find step-by-step folding instructions on page 10.

Fabrics: "Ivy" coordinates from VIP from Cranston.

Folds held in glasses expose both sides of the napkin. A lined style like the one shown here is worthy of the exposure. As a sidelight of napkin making, Gail collects funky vintage dishes, such as these once used at St. Mary School in Aberdeen, Washington – where she also happens to volunteer as a computer repairperson.

Terrific Topstitched Tubes

Avoid edge finishing altogether with another self-lined scheme. After turning the simple tube, stabilize and decorate the edges with one or more topstitching rows.

Five Easy Steps

1. Carefully cut out the rectangles. The rectangle corners should all be true right angles (90°), so the napkin tube will lie flat when seamed. Larger rectangles will yield larger napkins. (A)

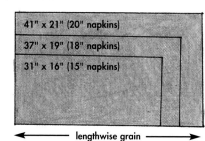

A

41" x 21" (20" napkins)

37" x 19" (18" napkins)

31" x 16" (15" napkins)

← lengthwise grain →

2. Fold the rectangle in half lengthwise, with right sides together. Straight stitch using a ½" seam allowance. Leave a 2" to 3" opening in the center for turning right side out later. (B)

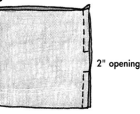

B

2" opening

3. Stitch the two ends, using a ½" seam allowance and wrapping the corners. (C)

4. Turn the napkin right side out through the opening. Press.

5. From the unseamed side of the napkin, topstitch ¼", ½", and ¾" (or as desired) from the napkin edges. Topstitching will keep the top and lining layers aligned through use and laundering. (D)

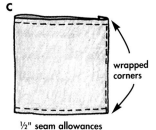

C

wrapped corners

½" seam allowances

Variations

Instead of topstitching, sew flat, washable trim, such as grosgrain, to the right side of the napkin, about ½" to 1" from the finished edges. Fold to miter the corners. (E)

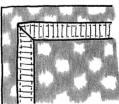

D

E

Featured Materials

- *Fabrics.* Any light- to medium-weight, tightly woven cotton, cotton blend, or other natural fiber fabric. Using 44"/45" fabric, 1¾ yards will yield six 15" napkins, 2¼ yards will yield four 18" napkins, and 2½ yards will yield four 20" napkins. For the best yield, cut the longer side of the rectangle parallel with the lengthwise grain of the fabric.

Flair

Find step-by-step folding instructions on page 10.

Fabrics: "Aunt Grace Signature Collection" from Marcus Brothers Textiles.

We trimmed the edges with grosgrain ribbon to define the napkin edges, add drama to the fold, and coordinate with this Lenox china. As a finishing touch, sometimes you get lucky, as Mary did, and find a napkin ring that matches the print motif.

Fast-Framed Finish

Frame your napkin in fabric, fast. Folding, hemming, and pressing get the job done, resulting in a border that is perfectly even every time, and a napkin that's perfectly flat for easier folding.

Four Easy Steps

1. Using our template system (see page 116), carefully cut out two squares for each napkin: one 21" square from the main fabric and one 19" square from a contrasting color. The finished napkin square will be 2" smaller than the larger unfinished square. (A)

2. On the larger square, miter fold 1" to the wrong side. Miter fold the smaller square ½" to the wrong side. (B)

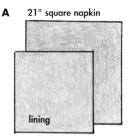

A 21" square napkin

lining

19" square

B napkin

1"

1"

lining ½"

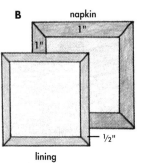

second fold first fold 1"

1" 1"

miter fold

third fold on this line

3. Center the smaller square over the larger square with wrong sides together. Leave an even border around the edges, about ½" wide (or whatever uniform border width allows the napkin to lie flat). Pin every 4" or so to secure the position for edgestitching. Using a small ruler (such as a 6" sewing gauge) speeds measuring and ensures accuracy. (C)

4. Thread your sewing machine with top thread that matches the lining and bobbin thread that matches the larger napkin "border." Edgestitch the lining to the napkin, pivoting at the corners.

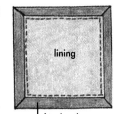

C

lining

½" border

Variations

For a firmer border when using lighter weight fabrics, fuse the hem of the larger napkin square, using ⅞" wide fusible web strips such as Therm O Web HeatnBond Lite. Miter fold the smaller square, without fusing. Proceed with Steps 3 and 4. (D)

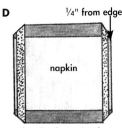

D ¼" from edge

napkin

fuse for firmer border

Featured Materials

- *Fabrics.* Any light- to medium-weight, tightly woven cotton, cotton blend, or other natural fiber fabric. We recommend an unfinished square size of 21" for the napkin and 19" for the lining. Using 44"/45" wide fabric, 1⅛ yards of the main napkin color will yield four 21" squares and 1⅛ yards of the lining color will yield four 19" squares.

  Note: *If you vary the size, remember to cut the lining square 2" smaller than the napkin square.*

- *All-purpose thread* to match both the napkin (for the bobbin) and the lining (for the top spool) fabrics. We recommend that you test stitch on scraps of the napkin and lining fabrics, wrong sides together. Balance the tension and shorten the stitch length so that neither thread shows on the opposite side.

Find step-by-step folding instructions on page 11.

Fabrics: "Bali Batiks" from Hoffman California International Fabrics.

You may have noticed this napkin on the book's cover too. It was the first one sewn for this book. We chose cotton batik because it's reversible, comes in a rich color range, and is universally available. The subtly marbled surface not only blends beautifully with any décor, it also hides wrinkles. We say, "If in doubt, choose cotton batik for napkins."

Fail-Proof Fused & Stitched Binding

Here's the best-looking, fastest binding around. Fusing stabilizes the binding and adds body to the napkin edge, while guaranteeing perfectly aligned, continuous edgestitching.

Four Easy Steps

1. Carefully cut out the napkin squares, using our template system (see page 116). Don't precut the binding into napkin-size lengths. Instead, cut to length after applying the binding (see Step 4).

2. Starting at the middle of one side, wrap the napkin edge with the fusible binding, equally dividing the binding width on both sides. Finger press. Fuse in place with the tip of your iron or a Mini Iron. Fuse to the corner, as shown. (A)

3. Wrap the corner with the binding, folding the miter. If needed, use a long pin to arrange the miter fold at a 45° angle. Press. Continue wrapping the edges and corners

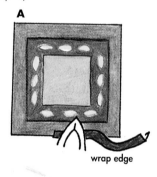

wrap edge

until the napkin is completely bound. (B)

4. Overlap the binding about 1" and trim to length. Turn under the raw edge about ½" and press, aligning the binding edges. Starting an inch or so away from the overlap, edgestitch the binding in place, pivoting at the corners. (C)

Variations

No time to sew? Bind the edges, use the napkins, and then edgestitch (Step 4) before laundering.

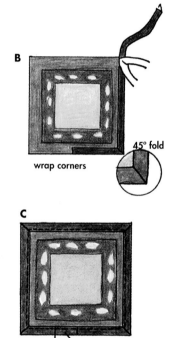

B

wrap corners

45° fold

C

fold under ½"

begin edgestitching

Featured Materials

- *Fabrics.* Just about any cotton, cotton blend, or other natural fiber fabric.
- *Fusible bias binding.* ¾" wide, 6½ yard roll (we used Clover Border Bias). For most 15" to 18" napkins, you'll need about 2⅛ yards per napkin, so a 6½ yard roll will hem about three napkins, a 5 yard package will hem about two napkins, and a 3 yard package will hem one napkin. To estimate, multiply four times the side measurement of the unfinished napkin, plus 1" for joining. Check yardage availabilities and price before deciding on a binding. Or, for better bias binding yields, decrease the size of your napkin slightly.

Note: *Any nonfusible bias binding, such as Wrights Extra Wide Bias Tape, can be a fusible: Center and fuse fusible web strips to the wrong side (see options on page 42), as well as 5 mm Clover Fusible Web. Or use the Clover Fusible Tape Maker. For the least expensive (but more time-consuming) bias-binding strips, cut and press your own (see page 118).*

Bouquet

Find step-by-step folding instructions on page 11.

Fabrics: "Bird Tree" from Springs' Quilters Only. Binding: Clover Border Bias.

Preprinted pillow patterns are perfect for napkins. The borders are already mitered and the size range is the same – about 15" to 20" square. Because the wrong side of the napkin would show in the Bouquet fold, we chose a coordinating lining too. The layers were fused together before the edges were bound. We're both sold on the easy accuracy of this binding method.

Fabrics: Left - "Farmer's Market" (check) by FreeSpirit and "Mirage with Glitter" by Fabric Traditions; right - "Aprons" from Michael Miller Fabrics.

Round, Fast-Fused Napkins

Simply cut out circles of fabric (see page 117). We recommend an unfinished diameter of 21". Apply the paper-backed fusible web strips as instructed on page 42, with the following changes. Working in 4" segments, use one continuous strip, shaping it to the curve by forming shallow folds in the paper.

When fusing, press inch-by-inch, easing in any extra hem fullness. Because there are no corners, this is a perfect finish for continuous machine stitching or trim application.

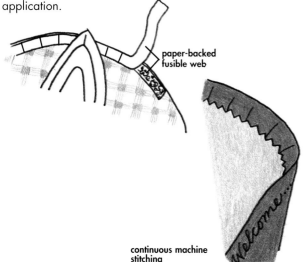

paper-backed fusible web

continuous machine stitching

Lined, Fast-Fused Napkins

Cut out a napkin 19" square, and a lining 18" square. We recommend using fabrics no heavier than "quilt" weight. Center the lining on the napkin, wrong sides together. Proceed with Steps 2 through 4 on page 42. *Optional:* Topstitch 3/8" from all edges, turning at the corners.

19" square

18" square

fusible web

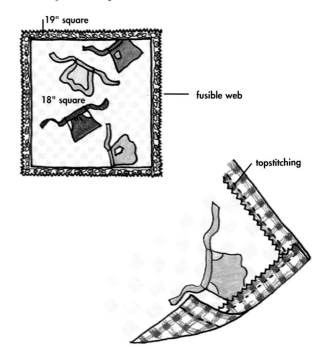

topstitching

Chapter 4

Machine-Sewn in Minutes

Fabrics: "Mirage with Glitter" (solid) and "Picnic Lunch" (print) from Fabric Traditions.

Recently a friend of Gail's announced, "I can't make napkins because I don't own a serger." That's a widespread but wrong assumption, and this chapter proves it. Whether your sewing machine is a lockstitch-only heirloom, or the latest machine embroidery model, turn to these tested techniques – no serger required (go to pages 79 to 88 for that).

A Quick Classic: Lined & Reversible

Double the weight, durability, and color options with this easy-sew napkin. The lining seams are wrapped, for the neatest, smoothest corners ever – and no trimming whatsoever.

Four Easy Steps

1. Carefully cut out the napkin squares, using our template system (see page 116). For each napkin, cut a top and lining square. (A)

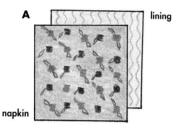

2. Start stitching the edges of the fabrics, as shown, turning at the seamline. Continue stitching with a ¼" seam allowance, off the fabric. (B)

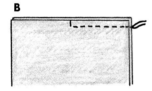

3. Wrap the corner by lifting the presser foot and folding the seam allowance along the seamline. Stitch the next side through all layers using a ¼" seam allowance. Repeat for the other sides and corners. Leave a 2" to 3" opening to turn the napkin right side out. Pivot and stitch

to the edges of the fabrics, which enhances the durability of the opening and the neatness of the interior seams. (C)

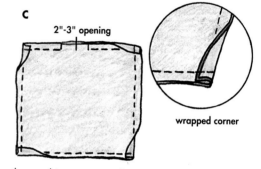

4. Press the napkin seams and corners. (Clipping the corner seams isn't necessary.) Turn the napkin right side out. Press, aligning the seam along the outer edges. Topstitch ¼" to ½" from all the edges, matching the top and bobbin threads to the napkin and lining. (D)

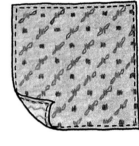

Variations

Stitch a buttonhole in one corner of the napkin, as shown on page 66. Or add additional rows of topstitching parallel to the first row stitched.

Featured Materials

- *Fabrics.* Any light- to medium-weight, tightly woven cotton, cotton blend, or other natural fiber fabric. Cut two squares for each napkin. We recommend an unfinished square size of 20½" for a finished size of 20". Using 44"/45" wide fabric, two ⅞ yard pieces will yield four 20½" squares for the top and four for the lining. For other yardages and sizes, see page 117.

Peaks Peeking

Find step-by-step folding instructions on page 12.

Fabrics: "Thimbleberries Sunshine & Shadows" from RJR Fashion Fabrics.

We wondered at first: "Does this fold look too imprecise?" In an effort to stage folding results more true-to-real-life, our conclusion was that the uneven layers didn't detract at all from the dramatic overall look. Plus, folding the napkin off-point exposed the lining. We're betting you will agree.

Pretty Hems, Painless Miters

For centuries, miters have graced the corners of napkins. Try our new angle on this old favorite: bias-cut napkins with mitered corners anyone can master.

Four Easy Steps

1. Carefully cut out bias napkin squares, using our template system (see page 116) on the fabric, as shown. (A) **Note:** *This napkin can be cut out more economically on the straight-of-grain, but we like the refreshing lines and angles of bias.*

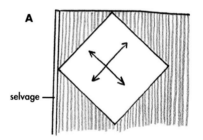

2. On the wrong side of the fabric, use a ruler to mark a line 1¼" from each edge on all four sides. Turn under and press ¼" on all four edges. (B)

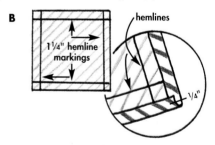

3. Fold-mark the miters. Fold the corner right sides together so the raw edges align. Fold the corner triangle down into the hem area. Use the diagonal fold line as a guide to draw a line to the folded edge. Pin the fabrics together and sew on the line, backstitching over the folded edges. Trim the seam allowances to minimize bulk. (C)

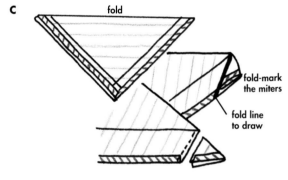

4. Finger press the seam open and turn the corner right side out. Repeat for the other corners. Topstitch the hems along the folded under edges. (D)

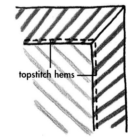

Variations

Instead of turning under the hem edges (Step 3), finish with pinking, zigzagging, or serging. Or fold rather than stitch the miters (see page 48).

Featured Materials

- *Fabrics.* Any light- to medium-weight, tightly woven cotton, cotton blend, or other natural fiber fabric. Cut one square for each napkin. We recommend an unfinished square size of 22½" for a finished 20" square. Using 44"/45" wide fabric, 2½ yards will yield four unfinished 22½" bias squares. For other sizes and yardages, see page 117.

Banana Peel

Find step-by-step folding instructions on page 12.

Fabric: "Red on Red! Kiss the Cook" from Dan River.

Mary has gathered quite a collection of wonderful hand-woven textiles, some loomed by talented artisans around Aurora, Minnesota. The topper under the red plate is a vintage linen towel she picked up at an estate sale. We encourage you to decorate eclectically, adding remembrances of friends, family, and travel to your new napkin settings.

Narrow, Nice & Simple: Twice-Turned Hems

Simply elegant, this lightweight finish can be straight stitched with any machine model – vintage to contemporary. Pressing "north-south, east-west" is prescribed, preventing corner jam-ups.

Four Easy Steps

1. Carefully cut out the napkin squares, using our template system (see page 116).

2. Using a dry iron (steam can burn your fingers!), press under ¼" on two opposite sides (north to south). Turn each edge under another ¼".

Note: *We usually "eyeball" to estimate the ¼" width, checking intermittently with a small ruler.* (A)

3. Repeat Step 2 for the two remaining edges (east to west). If the corners seem bulky, use sharp, small scissors to trim away some of the excess fabric that is turned inside. (B)

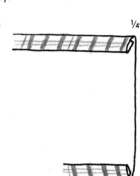

A   ¼"

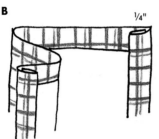

B   ¼"

4. Secure the hems with a few pins. From the right side, stitch the hems, about ⅛" in from the finished edge. *Do not start stitching at a corner, which can cause jamming.* At the corners, stitch slowly and pivot, then continue to stitch on the next side. (C)

Variations

Instead of straight stitching, choose utilitarian or decorative machine stitching to hem the edges. Favorites of ours are blanket stitching and triple zigzagging. (D) Or add emphasis with contrasting color thread.

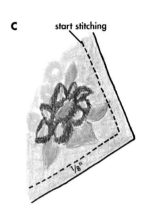

C   start stitching

⅛"

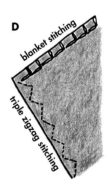

D   blanket stitching

triple zigzag stitching

machine stitch variations

Featured Materials

• *Fabrics.* Any light- to medium-weight, tightly woven cotton, cotton blend, or other natural fiber fabric. Cut one square for each napkin. We recommend an unfinished square size of 20" to 22" for a finished size of 19" to 21". Using 44"/45" wide fabric, 1¼ yards will yield four 20" to 22" squares. For other sizes and yardages, see page 117.

Rolled Flair

Find step-by-step folding instructions on page 13.

Fabrics: "Vintage Chic" prints and plaids from Dan River.

To complement these napkins, Gail dusted off all sorts of orphan dishes such as the decorative tray shown here. She's uncertain where this or the others came from, but was urged by Mary to combine unused pieces with coordinating napkins as gift sets. Great idea.

Double-Needle Delights

What an easy, intriguing hemming technique: The double needle forms two perfectly parallel rows of stitching. The single bobbin thread zigzags between the two top threads, minimizing raveling on the hem side of the napkin.

Four Easy Steps

1. Carefully cut out the napkin squares, using our template system (see page 116) and pinking shears or a pinked-blade rotary cutter. Press under 1" hems on two opposite sides of the square. (A)

2. Insert the double needle in the sewing machine. Thread with two spools, with each spool turning an opposite direction. Practice stitching on scrap fabric, holding the two top threads taut behind the presser foot as you begin stitching. (B)

A

1" hems

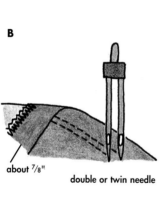

B

about ⅞"

double or twin needle

3. On the right side of the napkin, about ⅞" from the edge, stitch to hem each of the folded edges.

4. Turn under 1" and press the two remaining edges. Fold-miter the corners (see page 48), then stitch them. Backstitch one or two stitches at the beginning and end of the stitching. If the stitches look too messy with backstitching, adjust for a very short (.5) stitch. (C)

C

fold-miter corners and hem

Variations

Vary the stitch setting, as we did with the utilitarian stitches shown here. (D) The more detailed the stitch, the more weight is added to the edge and the more sewing time is required.

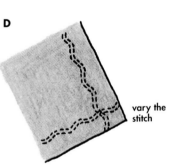

D

vary the stitch

Featured Materials

- *Fabrics.* Any light- to medium-weight, tightly woven cotton, cotton blend, or other natural fiber fabric. Cut one square for each napkin. We recommend an unfinished square size of 20" to 22" for a finished 18" to 20" square. Using 44"/45" wide fabric, 1¼ yards will yield four 20" to 22" squares. For other sizes and yardages, see page 117.
- *Double or twin needle.* We used a size 4.0 for the stitching. Widths now range from 1.6 mm to a super-wide 8 mm, in a full range of needle sizes from 11/75 to 16/10 (not all sizes fit all machines). The more lightweight the fabric, the finer the needle should be.
- *Zigzag sewing machine* that threads from the front to the back.
- *Pinking shears or pinked-blade rotary cutter.*

Bordered Fan

Find step-by-step folding instructions on page 13.

Fabrics: "Metallic Texture" from Concord House.

"Lining" with a second napkin is such a versatile folding strategy. For a more casual look, the blue napkin can be combined with a floral print. In this offset fold, the gold napkin also hides the wrong side of its blue counterpart. The ring here was another craft store bargain – a candle wreath.

Beautiful Borders

Used and laundered again and again, this substantial napkin maintains its shape and dramatic border design. Double your production of this design, then diagonally position the second set as matching placemats under the plates.

Four Easy Steps

1. Press the top and lining fabrics wrong sides together and carefully cut them out, using our template system (see page 116). For each napkin, cut a top and lining square and two trim strips. (A)

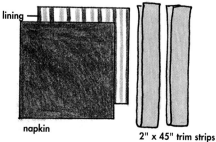

A

lining

napkin

2" x 45" trim strips

2. Turn under and press ¼" along one long edge of each fabric strip. Pin the raw edge of the fabric strip to the edge of the lined square, as shown, cutting the strips ¼" away from each end of the napkin fabrics. Stitch the strips to the napkin using ¼" seam allowances. (B)

B

lining

3. Press the seams, then fold and press the strip to the right side of the napkin. Pin the trim's folded edge in place and sew it to the napkin. Pin the raw edge of the strip to the edge of the remaining two sides of the napkin, planning for a ½" extension of fabric beyond the napkin edges. Sew the strips to the napkin edges, press, and turn the trim to the right side of the napkin. (C)

4. Turn under the fabric extensions to meet the napkin edges. If the edges are too thick or bulky, cut away the excess fabric. Pin and topstitch the last two trim edges to the napkin front. (D)

½" extension

C

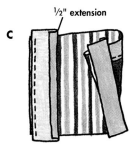

D

Variations

Substitute grosgrain or other flat, washable ribbon for the trim strips. Overlap the ends and stitch, as shown. (E)

E

variation: ribbon trim

Featured Materials

- *Fabrics.* Any light- to medium-weight, tightly woven cotton, cotton blend, or other natural fiber fabric. Cut two squares (one top and one lining) for each napkin. We recommend an unfinished square size of 20" for a finished 19" square. Using 44"/45" wide fabric, 1¼ yards will yield four 20" to 22" squares. For other sizes and yardages, see page 117. For the trim, cut two 2" x 45" strips for each napkin.
- *All-purpose thread* to match both the lining (bobbin) and the trim (top spool) fabrics.

Pocket

Find step-by-step folding instructions on page 14.

Fabrics: "Picnic Lunch" and "Mirage with Glitter," both from Fabric Traditions.

Although these fabrics weren't designed as coordinates, Mary trimmed the navy floral with the glitter-flecked lime border. Our guess is that you have prints, solids, and plaids stashed away that would be similarly stunning mixed together as napkins. Combine with abandon and delight in your innovative dining décor.

Clever Corded Wonder

Need a narrow finish for fabrics beefy enough to be used single layer? Try this hem-and-stitch strategy. Fine cording adds body and stability to the edge, while providing a "handle" for jam prevention at the corners.

Four Easy Steps

1. Carefully cut out the napkin squares, using our template system (see page 116).

2. Adjust your sewing machine for a wide, medium-length zigzag stitch. Start zigzagging over two strands of the cording, then on to the edge of the napkin. *Do not trim the cording tails.* Pull the cording tails as necessary to prevent jamming. Repeat on the opposite edge. (A)

3. Press the edges to the wrong side, close to the zigzagging. With a blanket or other utility stitch, stitch over the folded edge, using the cording to prevent jamming. Trim off the cording tails after stitching. (B)

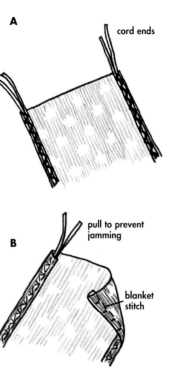

A

cord ends

B

pull to prevent jamming

blanket stitch

4. Repeat Steps 2 and 3 for the remaining two opposite sides of the napkin. Rather than backstitching at the beginning and end, stitch in one place. Dab with seam sealant and trim off all the tails when dry. (C)

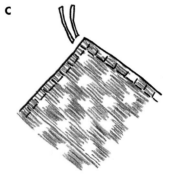

C

Variations

On smooth surfaced fabrics, test this technique first. If utility stitching is too bulky for your fabric, substitute straight stitching for the utility stitching in Step 3. (D)

Featured Materials

- *Fabrics.* Any medium-weight, firmly woven or surface-textured cotton, cotton blend, or other natural fiber fabric. Yarn and piece dyes work well because the wrong side is exposed. Cut one square for each napkin. We recommend an unfinished square size of 20" to 22" for a finished size of 19" to 21". Using 44"/45" wide fabric, 1¼ yards will yield four 20" to 22" squares. For other sizes and yardages, see page 117.
- *Cording.* Any washable, colorfast heavier thread, such as topstitching or buttonhole twist, or fine yarn, works well. On light-colored fabrics, the cording might show through, so choose accordingly. Otherwise, matching isn't crucial.
- *Sewing machine* with zigzag and utilitarian or decorative stitch capability. (We used blanket stitching on the sample.)

Find step-by-step folding instructions on page 14.

Napkins that are quietly themed can be used throughout the year. With a star motif fabric and the Early American fold, celebrate a specific patriotic holiday, such as Independence Day. Later, accessorize your table and restyle the fold for a different occasion or everyday dining.

Fabrics: "Bandanna Classic" and "Oh So Breit" from VIP by Cranston.

Buttonhole Corner Napkin

Follow the instructions for our Quick Classic: Lined and Reversible napkin on page 54. Before turning the napkin right side out, press mark a diagonal line on one corner. Fuse a 3" strip of paper-backed fusible web 3½" away from the corner, centered on the diagonal press marking.

Turn the napkin right side out, press the corners, and reach inside to remove the web's paper backing. Then press and fuse the fabric layers together (this is where the buttonhole will be stitched).

Mark a 2" buttonhole location on the diagonal pressed line. Stitch the buttonhole and cut it open. Then have some fun pulling the corners through the buttonhole and creating clever napkin formations. It's perfect as a bun warmer (depending on the size of your buns).

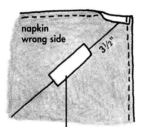

napkin
wrong side

3½"

paper-backed fusible web

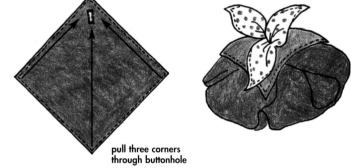

pull three corners
through buttonhole

Trimmed Edges

Follow the instructions for the Double-Needle Delights napkin on page 60. Instead of using the double needle, sew a single needle zigzag stitch to secure the 1" hems. Position the ribbon, flat braid, or bias tape over the zigzag stitching. Working opposite side-to-side, stitch the trim in place.

Fabric: Daisy Kingdom's "Glitter Gingham" by Springs. Trim: Clover Quick Fuse Bias.

Chapter 5
Quilt Lovers' Napkins

Fabrics: "The Old Glory Collection" from Marcus Brothers Textiles. Background quilt sewn by Nancy Zieman.

Quilters kept asking us for projects that would utilize their favorite fabrics and techniques, without the time and space demands of a full-size quilt. Keeping their wishes in mind, we developed these projects. Oh yes: You don't have to be a quilter to love the appealing – and practical – patchwork.

Fat Quarter Collection: Bias-Taped Borders

First, collect four fat quarter coordinates. Next, cut and combine the fabrics, adding narrow strips of bias for contrast and seam coverage. Then set a dramatic table, arranging the napkins into folds custom-designed for their shape.

Five Easy Steps

1. Trim away the selvage edges from all four fat quarters. Using our template system (page 116), cut each fat quarter to an 18" square. Save the remaining strip of fabric, which will be about 3½" x 18". (A)

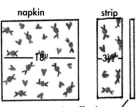

napkin   strip

18"

3½"

trim off selvage

2. Fold and press the strips in half lengthwise, with wrong sides together. Mix and match the strips to the 18" squares. Pin the raw edges to the wrong side of one of the square's edges. Sew together with a ¼" seam allowance. (B)

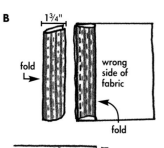

1¾"

fold

wrong side of fabric

fold

3. Press the seam allowances to one side, then trim the allowances to a scant ⅛" width. (C)

trim seam allowance

4. Cover the seam allowance with Clover Quick Bias and fuse in place. Straight stitch both edges of the bias in place. Other options for applying the bias tape include a triple-zigzag stitch or wide (4 mm) double-needle stitching. (D)

or triple zigzag stitch

5. Hem the remaining edges, starting with the edge opposite the border. Turn under the edge ¼" twice, pin, and straight stitch in place. Repeat for the two remaining edges. To decrease bulk in the area where the bias covers the seam allowance, trim some of the fabric and bias tape from the folded edge. (E) ***Note:*** *For the neatest hems, stitch from the top side of the napkin.*

trim to decrease bulk

Variations

Combine more than four different fabrics. Or add a second border to each napkin. (F)

variation: two borders

Featured Materials

- *Fat quarters.* Four different but coordinating prints are required. Any quilt-weight, tightly woven cotton fabric is recommended. The standard fat quarter size of 18" x 22" is used here.
- *Fusible bias tape.* Clover Quick Bias (¼" wide), one package (5.5 yards) to coordinate with all the fabrics. Or make your own (see page 118). To trim four napkins, you'll need 2¼ yards of bias.
- *"Invisible" nylon thread* or *all-purpose thread* to match the napkin fabrics.

Quilters' Heart

Find step-by-step folding instructions on page 15.

Fabrics: Mary Mulari's "Mother's Valentines" from Marcus Brothers Textiles. Quilt in background from Gail's collection.

Mary designed this fabric print, the napkin, and the ingenious Quilters' Heart fold. The Fat Quarter Collection (minus one) is displayed on one of Gail's heirloom quilts. In her hectic household, she would never risk using it as a table covering, but we've seen that done in trendy décor magazines.

Foundation Strips, Fast

There are minute-saving methods behind our quilting madness: cut or tear strips of fabric. Then stitch them to a foundation "base." The wider the strips, the faster the piecing. Finally, unify the piecing scheme with borders of "back-to-front" binding.

Four Easy Steps

1. Cut the 20" foundation fabric, using our template system (see page 116). Center an 18" template on the wrong side of the 20" fabric to mark an easy-to-see border. We recommend using wash-away marking pens or chalk markers. (A)

2. Start pinning and stitching the strips to the foundation, as shown. (B)

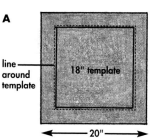

A

line around template

18" template

20"

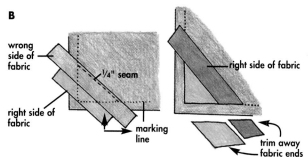

B

wrong side of fabric

1/4" seam

right side of fabric

marking line

right side of fabric

trim away fabric ends

Make sure that when the second fabric strip is lapped over the stitching line, it extends to the marked border on the foundation square. Trim away the excess fabric. Sew the strips to the foundation with a 1/4" seam allowance.

3. Continue to pin, stitch, press, and trim additional strips of fabric to the foundation until the foundation square is covered. (C)

4. Create the "back-to-front" binding. Fold two opposite foundation edges over 3/8" twice to the top side of the napkin. Straight stitch it in place, close to the inside folded edge of the binding. Repeat for the remaining two edges, as shown. (D) Also see Back-to-Front Binding, page 119.

Variations

Before binding, stitch strips of bias tape, rickrack, or other trim over some of the seams. Or cut one of the corner strips from inkjet copier fabric (see page 39). (E)

C

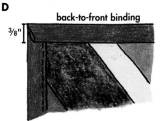

D

back-to-front binding

3/8"

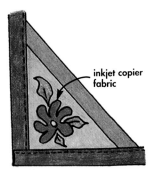

E

inkjet copier fabric

Featured Materials

- *Fabric for the foundation square.* Light- to medium-weight, tightly woven cotton, cotton blend, or other natural fiber fabric. We recommend a foundation square size of 20". Using 44"/45" wide fabric, 1⅛ yards of the main napkin color will yield four 20" squares.
- *Fabric for the piecing strips.* Assorted colors and/or prints to coordinate or contrast with the foundation square. We recommend 1" to 4" wide strips. The shortest strip length will be about 8", the longest will be about 27". (Don't precut the strips, see Step 2.)

Simple Pleat

Find step-by-step folding instructions on page 15.

Fabrics: "Bali Batiks" from Hoffman California International Fabrics.

Although some would say that quilting is strictly "country" décor, this vignette showed us otherwise. Notice the visual movement in all the elements: the piecing seams, the marbleized batik, and the fans. Gail calls it "Quilt Lovers' Napkins Go Far Eastern" – a classy look in just about any corner of the world.

Quick "Snowball" Corners

This traditional quilt corner takes on a new look in a napkin. "Snowballs" add weight and color emphasis, and with our template method, are simple to cut and stitch.

Four Easy Steps

1. For each napkin, use our template system (see page 116) to cut one 20" square (back side/binding), one 18" square (top side), and four 6" squares (snowball corners). (A)

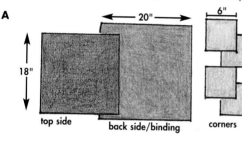

A
20"
6"
18"
top side   back side/binding   corners

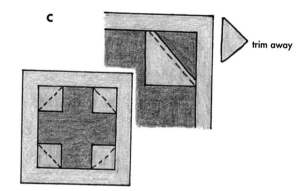

C
trim away

2. Center and pin the 18" square to the 20" square, with wrong sides together. (B)

3. Pin the 6" squares on each corner of the 18" square, with right sides together and aligning the edges. With a ruler and chalk marker or wash-away pen, draw a diagonal line from corner to corner on the 6" square. Straight stitch along the marked diagonal line. Repeat marking and stitching on the remaining three 6" squares. Trim away the corners of the 6" squares, as shown. (C)

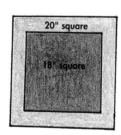

B
20" square
18" square

4. Create the "back-to-front" binding. Fold two opposite foundation edges over ³⁄₈" twice to the top side of the napkin. Straight stitch in place, close to the inside folded edge of the binding. Repeat for the remaining two edges, as shown. (D) Also see Back-to-Front Binding, page 119.

Variations

Select a different color or print for each snowball corner. (E)

D
³⁄₈"

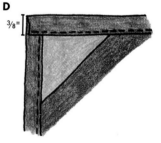

E

Featured Materials

• **Fabrics.** Any light- to medium-weight, tightly woven cotton, cotton blend, or other natural fiber fabric. We recommend a 20" square for the back side/binding, 18" for the top side, and 6" for the snowball corners. Using 44"/45" wide fabric, 1¹⁄₈ yards will yield four 20" squares, one yard will yield four 18" squares, and ¹⁄₂ yard will yield eight 6" squares.

Candle in a Cup

Find step-by-step folding instructions on page 16.

Fabrics: "Azalea Trail" coordinates from P & B Textiles.

Gail was quite puzzled about "snowball" corners. Why would Mary stitch snowball images on four corners of a harvest-hue print? When she saw the napkins, she understood: "Snowball" in quilting vernacular means the triangular corner piecing shown above. We couldn't resist adding Gail's cherished antique toy sewing machine to our snowball scene.

Four-Way Diagonal Napkins

Borrowing from quilters' diagonal piecing, this napkin is both fast to cut and fast to stitch. Mix and match fat quarters for charming napkin sets that can be folded and refolded to display four different fabric personalities.

Five Easy Steps

1. Place two pairs of two fabrics right sides together and use the template method (page 116) to cut the four squares simultaneously. For the "four-way" look shown, four different fabric squares are needed. (A)

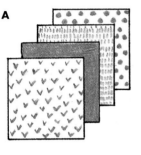

2. On the outer edges, pin two fabric squares wrong sides together. With chalk or wash-away marker, draw a diagonal line corner-to-corner on the wrong side of the top napkin square. (B)

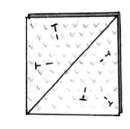

3. Straight stitch on each side of the diagonal line, using a ¼" seam allowance. Cut along the line drawn on the fabric to create two pieced squares. (C)

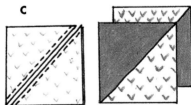

4. Repeat Steps 2 and 3 for the two remaining fabric squares.

5. Place the squares right sides together, alternating the pieced seams at the corners, as shown. (D) Seam the two squares together as shown on page 54 for Lined and Reversible Napkins. Turn right side out. *Optional:* For a more defined edge, edgestitch around the napkin. (E)

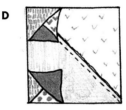

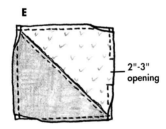

2"-3" opening

Variations

To save time, cut one unpieced square for the napkin lining. (F)

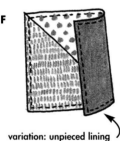

variation: unpieced lining

Featured Materials

- **Fabrics.** Any light- to medium-weight, tightly woven cotton, cotton blend, or other natural fiber fabric. We recommend 18" or 20" squares of two fabrics for each napkin. Using 44"/45" wide fabric, 1⅛ yards will yield four 20" squares and one yard will yield four 18" squares. Four fat quarters (18" x 22" each) will yield four 18" squares. **Note:** The instructions above will yield two napkins, combining four fabrics.

Trumpet Garden

Find step-by-step folding instructions on page 16.

Fabrics: "Cambridge Common" and "Color Connectors" by FreeSpirit Fabrics. Quilt designed and sewn by Lorrie Walsh.

Achieve stunning results by mixing fabrics in unexpected ways — such as piecing this brighter red with the subtle toiles. The quilt backdrop is made from a linen tablecloth, signed by guests at a family cabin. At 18, while visiting her college boyfriend there, Gail signed it; she married her date 17 years later.

More Fat Quarter Bounty: Bias Borders

From Mary's bountiful bag of fat quarter tricks comes another resourceful scheme: Cut four 18" napkins and use the leftover fabric for bias-border trim.

Six Easy Steps

1. Trim away the selvage edges from all four fat quarters. Use our template system (see page 116) to cut each fat quarter to an 18" square. Save the remaining strip of fabric, which will be about 3½" x 18". (A)

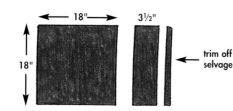

A

<- 18" -> 3½"

18"

trim off selvage

2. Using a ¼" seam allowance and short straight stitch, sew the four strips of fabric together, in stair steps. Place the end of each fabric strip 3½" beyond the adjoining strip, as shown. (B)

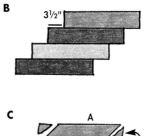

B

3½"

3. Press the seam allowances in one direction, then press the napkin. Draw a straight line on the stepped edges, then cut off the extending corners. (C)

C

A

B

sew edge A to edge B

trim off corners

4. Align the edge of the top fabric to the edge of the bottom fabric, right sides together. This feels awkward but works! Using ¼" seam allowances and a short stitch length, stitch the seam. The fabric strips are now a tube. Press the seam allowances in one direction. (D)

D

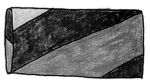

5. Cut the tube into four equal segments. Each tube should be cut open in a different fabric section. Turn under and press the long raw edges of each fabric band and position them 1" inside the napkin edge. Pin intermittently and straight stitch in place. (E)

E

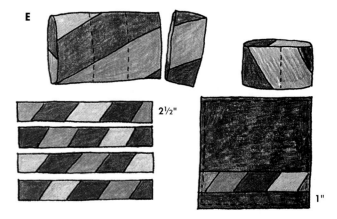

2½"

1"

6. To hem the napkin edges, turn under two opposite edges ¼" twice and pin. Repeat for the two remaining sides. From the right side, straight stitch the hems in place, about ¼" from the edge.

Variations

Cut out the 18" squares from the same color fabric, and the border from four different fabrics (not including the main color).

Featured Materials

- *Fat quarters.* Four different, coordinating prints are required. The standard fat quarter size of 18" x 22" of each print will yield four 18" napkins.

Forget-Me-Knot

Find step-by-step folding instructions on page 17.

Fabrics: "Old Glory" coordinates by Marcus Brothers Textiles. Quilt in background sewn by Nancy Zieman.

The beauty of color blending became apparent when we were assembling plates, backgrounds, and pieced napkins. You'll discover the same decorating magic when setting your table – somehow, everything looks as though it was made to go together.

Fabrics: "Contemporary Christmas" from Concord House Fabrics.

Fabrics: "Homespun Plaids" from VIP by Cranston, and "Thimbleberries Sunshine & Shadows" from RJR Fabrics.

Fat Quarter Banner Napkins

Put these banners to work as napkins or placemats. A roll-up fold shows off the tapered end (see Roll Call on page 17).

Cut out two 18" squares from yardage or fat quarters. Trace the banner shape on the wrong side of one square. Stitch the two napkins together with a ¼" seam allowance, leaving a 3" opening for turning right side out. Turn right side out and press.

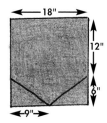

wrong side of fabric

Variation

Use the entire fat quarter to make a larger banner napkin or placemat.

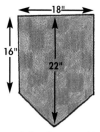

variation: larger napkin or placemat

Stitched-On Bound Edge

Stitched-on binding is reversible and surprisingly tidy on this quilt-look preprinted panel. Fuse the napkin and lining wrong sides together, using fusible web strips. Starting with the center of one side, wrap the edge with Wright's Double-Fold Bias Tape (½" wide). Straight stitch in place. Stitch off the corner, then wrap the corner to miter. Resume stitching, backstitching to secure. Repeat for the other corners. Finish by folding under ½" and stitching in place.

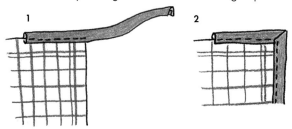

Quickly! Blanket Stitching

Add blanket-stitched accents along the inner or outer edge of a lined, fused edge napkin (see page 52).

blanket stitching variations

Chapter 6

Serged Napkins As Never Before

Fabrics: "Meow Magic" and "Color Connectors" from FreeSpirit Fabrics.

Gail has written five books and hundreds of articles about serging. You might wonder if the information has changed much, year to year. It has. We've all learned and expect more, while the machines, methods, and threads have improved – hence our title "... As Never Before."

Serged Standby: Turn & Topstitch

This tandem technique, both serged and conventionally stitched, was once snubbed by experts as too simple. Well, simple it is: simply convenient, tailored – and trouble-free.

Four Easy Steps

1. Carefully cut out the napkin squares, using our template system (see page 116). If you are new to serging and in doubt about size, go bigger: Then, if the edges are trimmed off in re-serging, the napkin won't be skimpy.

2. Set up for balanced tension, medium-width, medium-length three-thread serging. Refer to Serging: Gail's Tried and True Tips (page 115) and your serger manual. Just about any serger has this stitch capability. Test serge on scraps of your napkin fabric. Then serge-finish all the edges, trimming ⅛" to ¼" throughout. (A)

3. Press the ½" hems on all edges, folding to miter the corners. (B) For wider, weightier hems, press up to 1" hems along all the edges.

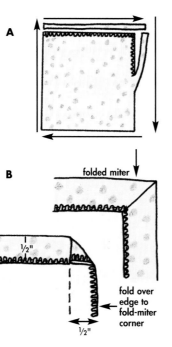

folded miter

½"

fold over edge to fold-miter corner

½"

4. From the right side, topstitch ⅜" from the napkin edge, pivoting at the corners. Backstitch to secure the end of the stitching. (C)

Variations

For additional weight and reversibility, line the napkin before serge-finishing. Use self-fabric or a care-compatible coordinate. After pressing the folded miters in the lined napkin, you may need to trim the layers inside the corner to decrease bulk. (D)

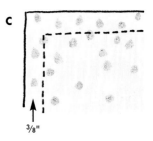

⅜"

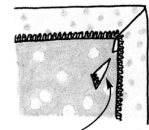

trim away to decrease bulk

Featured Materials

- *Fabrics*. Any light- to medium-weight, tightly woven cotton, cotton blend, or other natural fiber fabric. Cut one square for each napkin. We recommend an unfinished square size of 20" to 22" for a finished size of 18" to 21", depending on the trim and the hem width. Using 44"/45" wide fabric, 1¼ yards will yield four 20" to 22" squares. For other sizes and yardages, see page 117.
- *Serger/overlock* or *all-purpose thread* to match, for all positions.

Featured Fold   Peacock

Find step-by-step folding instructions on page 18.

Fabric: "Jane's Exotic Garden" from FreeSpirit Fabrics.

Because the wrong side of this napkin shows through the glass, we opted for lining (see Variations). Mary (also known in the sewing world as the "Appliqué Goddess") extracted the flower motif from the print coordinate shown on the table. The easy fold evolved, showing off the appliqué as would a preening peacock.

Quintessentially Napkins: Narrow-Rolled Edges

With no conventional stitch as lightweight or refined, narrow-rolled edging sold the sewing world on serging. Now, with the reliability and speed of our latest thread setup, you may want to devote a serger exclusively to this stitch – and napkins.

Five Easy Steps

1. Carefully cut out the napkin squares, using our template system (see page 116).

2. Using paper-backed fusible web strips ($\frac{1}{2}$" to $\frac{7}{8}$" wide) fuse together the napkin and the lining. (This is important because it stabilizes the edges for more uniform serged finishing.) (A)

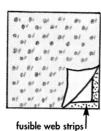

A

fusible web strips

3. Set up for a narrow-rolled edge, fine-tuning all the settings during testing. Use the right needle position. Adjust for or change to the narrow stitch finger. Narrow the stitch width (or "bite") to about 1. Shorten the stitch to about 1. Tighten the lower looper and loosen the upper looper so that it wraps the edge. The needle thread may also require some tightening. Rethread, using Woolly Nylon in all positions. Test serge on scraps of your napkin fabric.

4. Serge-finish all the edges, trimming about $\frac{1}{8}$" to $\frac{1}{4}$". Round the corners slightly, serging off and on. Dab with seam sealant, allow to dry, and trim off. (B)

5. For round or rounded napkins, start and finish serging in a notched out section, as shown. (C)

Variations

Center the rickrack under the rolled edge and straight stitch it in place along the serged needle line. (D)

B

trim off

round corners slightly

C

start and finish serging here

serger knife

$1\frac{1}{2}$"

D

rickrack stitched to napkin

Featured Materials

- *Fabric.* Any light- to medium-weight, tightly woven cotton, cotton blend, or other natural fiber fabric. Cut two squares or circles for each: one napkin and one lining. We recommend an unfinished square size of 18" to 22" for a finished size range of $17\frac{1}{2}$" to $21\frac{1}{2}$". Using 44"/45" wide fabric, $1\frac{1}{4}$ yards will yield four 20" to 22" squares. For other sizes and yardages, see page 117.

- *Woolly Nylon thread,* regular weight, or any similar multifilament nylon thread, to match or contrast, for all positions. Three cones.

- *Optional: Jumbo rickrack trim.* A $2\frac{1}{2}$ yard package is required for most napkin sizes. For more than one or two napkins, we recommend purchasing large rolls of rickrack, available through Home-Sew and other mail-order suppliers (see page 127).

Featured Fold

Potted Plant

Find step-by-step folding instructions on page 18.

Fabrics: Mary Englebreit's "Oh So Breit" coordinates from VIP by Cranston.

Designer Mary Englebreit had different projects in mind when she designed this preprinted fabric: the round napkin shown here was to be a placemat, and the pocket a coaster. The versatility of preprinted panels is multiplied with narrow-rolled serging because the stitch is hemless, efficiently maximizing the image size no matter how many curves or corners.

Wrapped-Edge Finish

Looking for a wider, more substantial rolled edge?
"Wrapping" is the answer, with a simple setup that showcases
yarns and other decorative threads adaptable to serging.

Four Easy Steps

1. Carefully cut out the napkin squares, using our template system (see page 116).

2. Using paper-backed fusible web strips (½" to ⅞" wide), fuse together the napkin and the lining. (This is important because it stabilizes the edges for more uniform serged finishing.) (A)

3. Set up for a wrapped edge, fine-tuning all the settings during testing. Use the left needle position and a standard stitch finger. Adjust for a medium-width stitch. Set for the longest stitch. Tighten the lower looper. Loosen the upper looper completely. (For

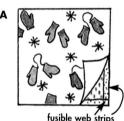

A
fusible web strips

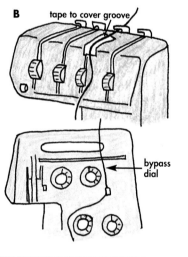

B
tape to cover groove

bypass dial

additional loosening, remove the yarn from one or more of the guides. (B)

The needle thread may also require tightening. Rethread, using Success in the upper looper and Woolly Nylon in the needle and lower looper. Test serge on scraps of your napkin fabric.

4. Serge-finish all the edges, trimming about ⅛" to ¼". Round the corners slightly, serging off and on. (C) Dab with seam sealant, allow to dry, and with a tapestry needle, weave the thread tails under the looper threads on the lining side. (D)

Variations

Use a contrasting color needle thread for interesting two-tone effects. See the napkin in the Mini-Mitten on page 22.

Featured Materials

- *Fabrics.* Any light- to medium-weight, tightly woven cotton, cotton blend, or other natural fiber fabric. Cut two squares for each: one napkin and one lining. We recommend an unfinished square size of 18" to 22" for a finished size range of 17½" to 21½". Using 44"/45" wide fabric, 1¼ yards will yield four 20" to 22" squares. For other sizes and yardages, see page 117.
- *Success Acrylic Serging Yarn,* to match or contrast, for the upper looper. Or any similar, strong, lightweight two-ply yarn. Two cones. You can substitute most needle-punch yarns, preferably on top- or side-feeding spools or cones.
- *Woolly Nylon thread.* Two cones of regular weight, to match the yarn, for the needle and lower-looper positions. Or any similar multifilament nylon thread.

Tied Ascot

Find step-by-step folding instructions on page 19.

Fabrics: Mary Mulari's "Knittin' Mittens" from Marcus Brothers Textiles. Serging yarn: Success Acrylic.

Warm any cool weather gathering with these whimsical, wrapped-edge napkins. The serged yarn finish seemed especially appropriate for this print design, inspired by Mary's growing collection of hand-knitted Scandinavian-style mittens. As a ring, a miniature pair is tied with an attached cord.

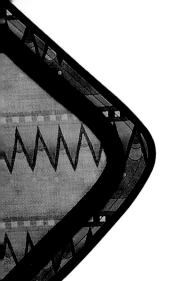

Sleek Serged Banding

So often we limit serging to edge finishes. But the wonderful action of trimming and overlocking simultaneously also makes exposed seaming possible, as in the case of this beautiful, unbulky banding.

Five Easy Steps

1. Carefully cut out the napkin squares using the template method (see page 116). Use a cup or special curve template such as the Radial Rule to round off the corners. (A)

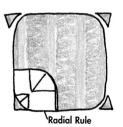

Radial Rule

2. Cut out the bias strips for the banding, 1½" wide. For a 19" napkin, you will need about 2⅛ yards of bias. Piece as necessary (see page 118).

3. Set up for balanced tension, medium-width, medium-length, three-thread serging, using all-purpose or serger thread. Test serge on scraps of your napkin fabric. Then serge-finish the edges of the napkins, barely skimming off the edge. (B) (Don't worry about perfect stitches – not much will show under the banding.)

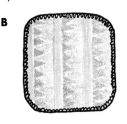

4. Fold and press the bias band in half, lengthwise. Straight stitch ⅜" from the

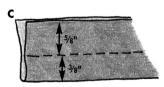

folded edge. Then serge-finish all the raw edges together, trimming off about ⅛". (C)

5. Starting in the center of one side, pin the edges of the banding to the napkin, overlapping the edges slightly so the napkin will be hidden under the banding. Straight stitch directly over the banding stitching line. Start and finish the banding treatment, as shown. Press the banding allowance under and topstitch ¼" from the seamline, as shown. (D)

Variations

Cut the napkins on the bias (see page 79, and the photo, right). (E)

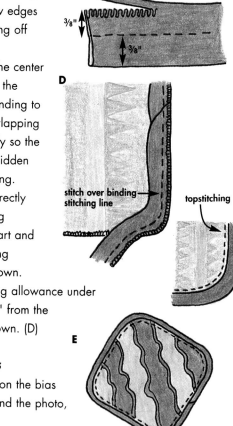

Featured Materials

- *Fabrics.* Any light- to medium-weight, tightly woven cotton, cotton blend, or other natural fiber fabric. Cut one square for each napkin. We recommend an unfinished square size of 18" to 21" for a finished, banded size range of 19" to 22" rounded-corner square. Using 44"/45" wide fabric, 1¼ yards will yield four 19" to 21" squares and one yard will yield four 18" squares. For other sizes and yardages, see page 117.
- *Fabric for bias banding,* in a contrasting color. For a set of four napkins, one yard of 44"/45" wide fabric will yield bias strips with minimal piecing seams. Or use less yardage and refer to our chart on page 118.

Victory

Find step-by-step folding instructions on page 19.

Fabrics: "Meow Magic" and "Color Connectors" from FreeSpirit Fabrics.

This napkin's banding is a perfect example of the exposed construction made possible with serging. Conventional and serged stitches, when combined, bring out the best in napkins: fast, flat, and foldable finishing anchored with durable lockstitching.

Fabric: "Fifth Avenue Designs" for Covington. Lace: Cluny lace from Home-Sew.

Fabric: "Sweetbriar" from Marcus Brothers Textiles.

Lapped-Trim Finish

Try this charming finish on decorator fabrics, or any fabric too heavy to be used double layer. (Launder later, after finishing, to remove any scratchy sizing.)

Adjust for medium-length and -width, balanced-tension serging and serge-finish the edges. Lap the lace or trim over the right side of the edge, covering the serging. With a sewing machine, edgestitch in place, folding to miter the corners. *Optional:* After stitching the miter, trim away the excess lace.

Narrow Serged and Turned

Want the body and durability of a hemmed edge without the weight? Use this narrowest of hems.

Adjust for medium-length and -width, balanced-tension serging and serge-finish the edges. Don't trim the thread tails. Press under the edge to the wrong side along the serged needle line (a scant ¼" or so). With a sewng machine and from the right side, edgestitch the hem in place. To prevent jamming at the corners, gently pull the thread tails.

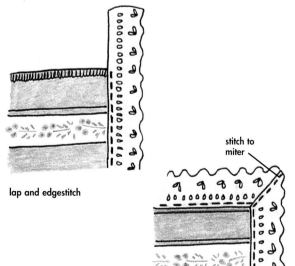

lap and edgestitch

stitch to miter

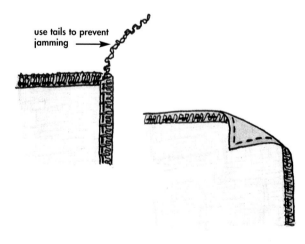

use tails to prevent jamming →

Chapter 7
Machine Embroidery Showcase

Think of napkins as perfect palettes for machine embroidery. Stitch a matching set, or use the same thread color as the unifying element and experiment with different stitches on every napkin. Whether you are a beginner or a pro, let the embroidered corners in this chapter be your inspiration.

Machine Embroidery Showcase

From Bernina of America

- **Design Card**: Austrian Laces design card and lettering built into Bernina sewing machines.
- **Thread**: Isacord thread, 40-weight.
- **Notes**: The lace design was stitched on one layer of Badgemaster water-soluble stabilizer. The initial was stitched on one layer each of polyester organza and Badgemaster. After the stabilizer was rinsed away, the lace was positioned and stitched on the napkin corner. Excess organdy fabric around the initial was melted away with a stencil-burning tool. The initial was stitched to the napkin with a narrow zigzag stitch and clear monofilament thread.
- **Tips**: For timesaving embroidery, duplicate the designs several times in a larger embroidery hoop.

Stitched by Jennifer Gigas

From Elna USA

- **Design Card**: Lace design built into the Elna Exquisit sewing machine.
- **Thread**: Finishing Touch Rayon, 35-weight.
- **Notes**: Finishing Touch Ultra Tear-Away was used as stabilizer. The napkin corner was held in place on the stabilizer with Sulky KK2000 temporary fusible spray.
- **Tips:** Soft, subtle colors of embroidery thread add a touch of class to white napkins.

Stitched by the Elna Education Staff

Designs from Sewing Machine Companies

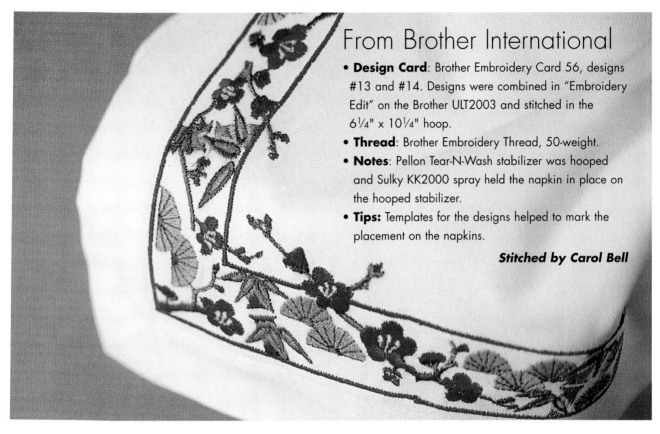

From Brother International

- **Design Card**: Brother Embroidery Card 56, designs #13 and #14. Designs were combined in "Embroidery Edit" on the Brother ULT2003 and stitched in the 6¼" x 10¼" hoop.
- **Thread**: Brother Embroidery Thread, 50-weight.
- **Notes**: Pellon Tear-N-Wash stabilizer was hooped and Sulky KK2000 spray held the napkin in place on the hooped stabilizer.
- **Tips:** Templates for the designs helped to mark the placement on the napkins.

Stitched by Carol Bell

From Babylock USA

- **Design card:** Babylock Exclusive Design card BLEC-C20 and design #9. Lettering is "Kids True Type" font used in Palette Software.
- **Thread:** Sulky Rayon thread, 40-weight.
- **Notes**: Tear-away stabilizer was hooped and 505 Temporary Adhesive Spray used on the back of the napkin corner to hold it in place.
- **Tips:** Napkins are a great idea for a special occasion such as a little boy's birthday party. Another idea: Let the party guests stitch their own napkins.

Stitched by Pamela Mahshie

Machine Embroidery Showcase

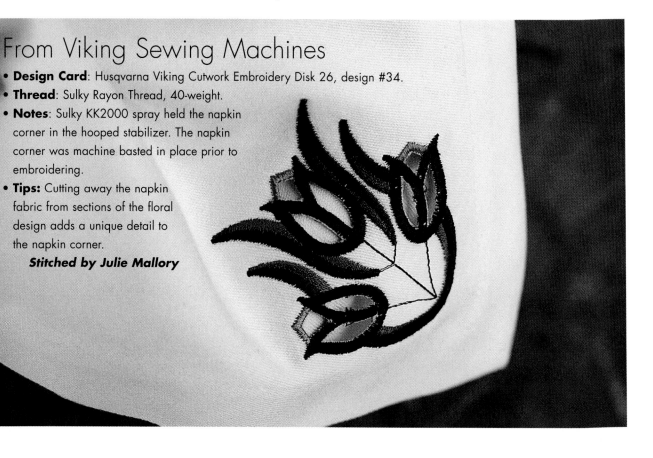

From Viking Sewing Machines

- **Design Card**: Husqvarna Viking Cutwork Embroidery Disk 26, design #34.
- **Thread**: Sulky Rayon Thread, 40-weight.
- **Notes**: Sulky KK2000 spray held the napkin corner in the hooped stabilizer. The napkin corner was machine basted in place prior to embroidering.
- **Tips:** Cutting away the napkin fabric from sections of the floral design adds a unique detail to the napkin corner.

   Stitched by Julie Mallory

From Janome

- **Design Card**: Janome Oriental Collection Card 1015, design #6.
- **Thread**: Robison-Anton thread, 40-weight.
- **Notes**: Two layers of Aqua Magic stabilizer were hooped for the embroidery. The napkin corner was pinned to the stabilizer.
- **Tips**: The napkin hem was embellished with 3 mm wide satin stitching accented with an additional row of triple straight stitching with Janome metallic thread.

   Stitched by Michele Mishler

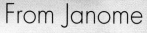

Designs from Sewing Machine Companies

From Pfaff American Sales Corp.

- **Design Card**: Pfaff Card 300, design #24.
- **Thread**: Robison-Anton Rayon Thread, 40-weight.
- **Notes**: Hydro-Stick stabilizer was hooped and moistened so the napkin could be positioned and held in place in the hoop. A design template temporarily laid inside the hoop was used to mark lines for positioning the napkin corner.
- **Tips**: The embroidery design and thread colors were chosen to coordinate with a china dinnerware pattern.

Stitched by Patricia Timms

From Singer Sewing Company

- **Design Card**: Poinsettia from Singer Sewing Card 20. Lettering from computer software.
- **Thread**: Robison-Anton Polyester Thread, 40-weight.
- **Notes**: Pellon Stitch 'N Tear Lite was chosen for the stabilizer and the napkin corner was pinned to the hooped stabilizer.
- **Tips**: Holiday embroideries on napkins add colorful accents to the dinner table. For variety, consider using different holiday designs on each napkin.

Stitched by Cheri Collins

Machine Embroidery Showcase

From Cactus Punch

- **Design Card**: Cactus Punch Card CC06, "Tea Time Appliqué."
- **Thread**: Sulky Rayon Thread, 40-weight.
- **Notes**: Aqua Magic stabilizer was hooped and Sulky KK2000 spray held the napkin corner in place, along with machine basting before embroidering.
- **Tips**: Appliqué designs save stitching time and thread since fabric covers areas that are stitched over in traditional embroidery. Tea parties are even more festive with theme-embellished napkins.

Stitched by Lindee Goodall

From Embroidery Arts

- **Design Card**: Embroidery Arts Diamond Monogram Set 4.

- **Thread**: Madeira Rayon Thread, 40-weight.
- **Notes**: Medium-weight tear-away stabilizer and the napkin were hooped together.
- **Tips**: Suggestions for accurate placement of monograms: Sew a sample and make a photocopy. Determine the exact center of the design and cut a small hole in the paper. Hoop the napkin with stabilizer and use the photocopied template to mark the center of the design on the napkin.

Stitched by Embroidery Arts

From Embroidery Design Companies

From Dakota Collectibles

- **Design Card**: Dakota Collectibles Presents "Gunold Fashion Heirloom Catalog," design #QHL01168.
- **Thread**: Madeira Rayon Thread, 40-weight.
- **Notes**: Aquafilm stabilizer was hooped and the napkin corner placed on top of the stabilizer, using KK100 Fabric Adhesive.
- **Tips**: When decorating several napkins, the single color design adds delicate, old world stitching detail to the napkin corner and saves time, with no thread color changes.

Stitched by Margo Vranna,
Dakota Collectibles Sewing Department

From Criswell Embroidery and Design

- **Design Card**: Petit Point Design Collection from Criswell Embroidery and Design, Bargello design.
- **Thread**: Madeira Rayon Thread, 40-weight.
- **Notes**: Two layers of Super Solvy water-soluble stabilizer were hooped and 505 Fusible Adhesive Spray held the napkin in place on the stabilizer.
- **Tips**: One design repeated three times in a napkin corner creates opportunities for rectangular or diagonal napkin folds.

Stitched by Judith Bunting

Machine Embroidery Design Companies

From Oklahoma Embroidery Supply (OESD)

- **Design Card**: OESD Licensed Collection 768, "Tassels and Trims" by Louisa Meyer.
- **Thread**: Isacord Polyester Embroidery Thread.
- **Notes**: Two layers of OESD Ultra Clean and Tear stabilizer were hooped, after they were sprayed together with 505 Temporary Adhesive Spray to prevent shifting during embroidery. Design templates were used to plan and position the design on the napkin.
- **Tips**: The threads of the tiny tassels add dimensional interest to the napkin corner.

Stitched by Kay Lynch

From Vermillion Stitchery

- **Design Card**: Christmas Alphabet CD.
- **Thread**: DMC thread, 50-weight.
- **Notes**: Stabilizer chosen was Viking Fuse 'n Tear and the napkin and stabilizer were hooped together.
- **Tips**: The design motif can be combined with letters for monograms to personalize holiday napkins. The design CD features versatile ways to combine cross stitch designs, letters, and Christmas themes.

Stitched by Laura Vermillion Himes

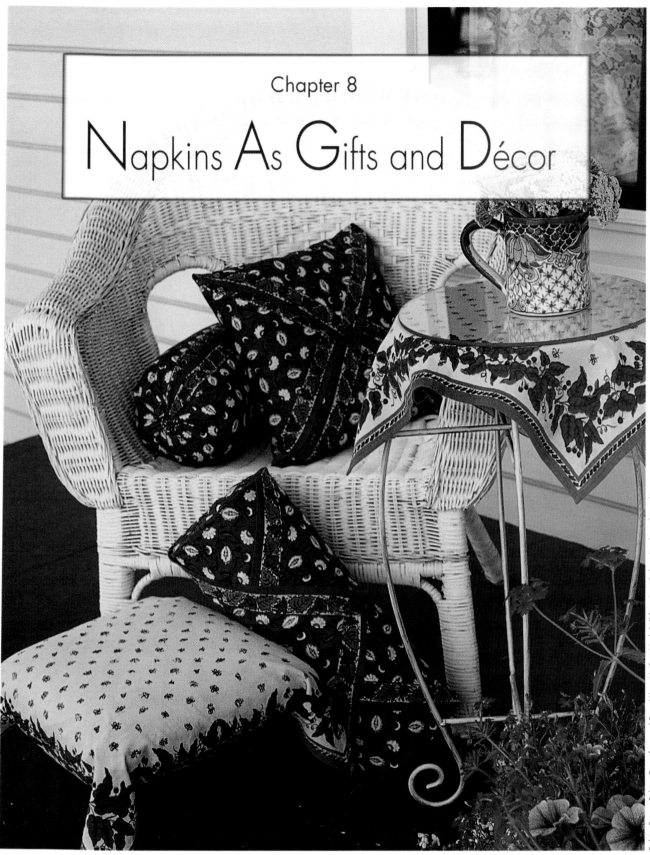

Chapter 8
Napkins As Gifts and Décor

Napkins assume surprising, practical identities away from the table. There's not a more versatile, reusable ingredient for instant interiors, accessories, or gifts.

As Seasonal Gift Sets

All fabrics: Fabric Traditions and FreeSpirit Fabrics: Spring, "Picnic Lunch," Summer, "Farmers' Market," Fall, "Fall Medley," Winter, "First Snowfall" and "Snowman Dance Party." Embroidery designs: Oklahoma Embroidery Supply & Design (OESD); Lettering stitched on Bernina Artista sewing machine.

What better gift than a seasonally themed set of napkins? Mary gives them to young couples, so they can dine together elegantly, even if on a card table. Dress up napkin gift sets with the new folds you've learned (see pages 7 to 30) and give them as a mixed or matched set.

As Gift Wrap or Presentations

Fabric: "Angels from Heaven" from Fabric Traditions.

Are your closets filled with orphan napkins or fabrics from unfinished projects? Put them to work as gorgeous gift wrap that is a gift in itself, usable again and again.

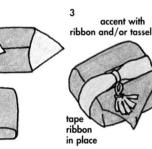

1
15"-22" napkin
3"-6" square

2
tape option

3
accent with ribbon and/or tassel
tape ribbon in place

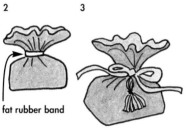

1
15"-22" circle
3"-5" square

2
fat rubber band

3
accent with ribbon and tassel

As "blooming" napkins

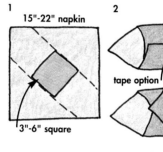

1
pick up center of napkin

2
4"
add rubber band

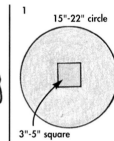

3
press in center with finger

4
accent with ribbon and/or tassel

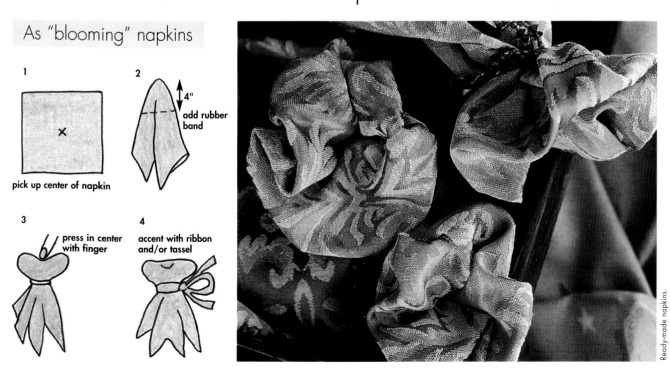

Ready-made napkins.

As Basket Fillers, Liners & Accents

As a buffet basket filler (with flatware)

Fold as shown on page 102, then arrange the roll-ups in a buffet basket.

Fabrics: "Aprons" from Michael Miller Fabrics.

As a blooming napkin basket

Mix colors and prints to create a fabric bouquet (for folding how-tos, see page 99).

Fabrics: Kari Pearson's "Rainbow Bright Basics" from Quilting Treasures by Cranston.

As a basket liner

Custom fit a round or square napkin liner by gathering in the center and securing it with a fat rubber band.

Fabric: "Farmers Market" by FreeSpirit Fabrics.

As a buffet napkin basket (without flatware)

Fold a set of napkins to fill a basket. This is the Victory fold (see page 19 for instructions).

Vintage bark cloth napkins from Gail's collection.

As Special Occasion Settings

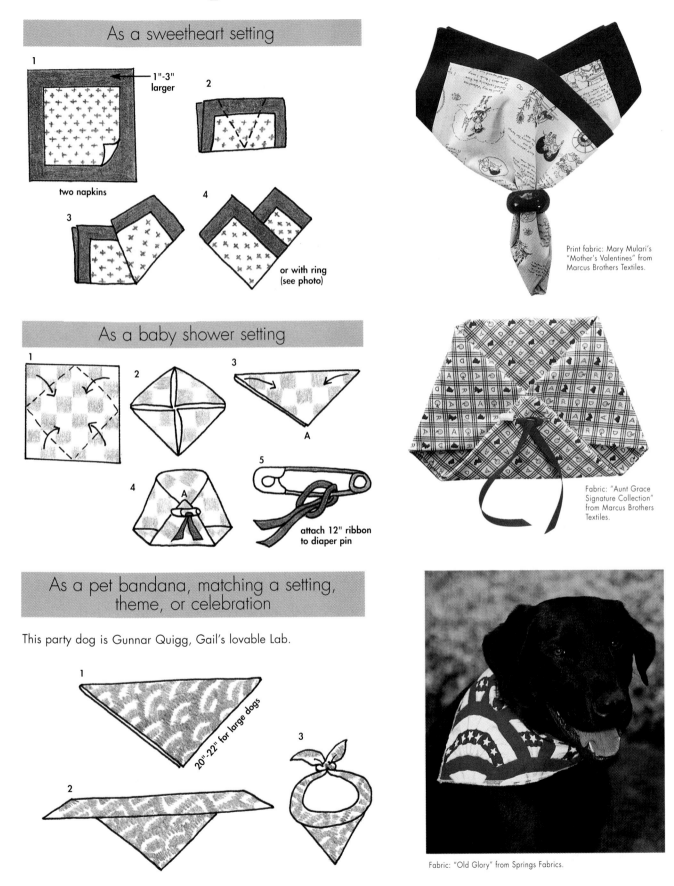

As a sweetheart setting

1
1"-3" larger

two napkins

2

3

4

or with ring
(see photo)

Print fabric: Mary Mulari's "Mother's Valentines" from Marcus Brothers Textiles.

As a baby shower setting

1

2

3

A

4

5

attach 12" ribbon
to diaper pin

Fabric: "Aunt Grace Signature Collection" from Marcus Brothers Textiles.

As a pet bandana, matching a setting, theme, or celebration

This party dog is Gunnar Quigg, Gail's lovable Lab.

1
20"-22" for large dogs

2

3

Fabric: "Old Glory" from Springs Fabrics.

As Other Table Linens

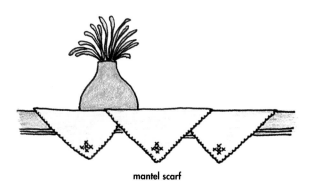

runner

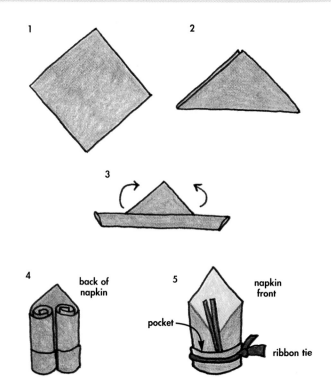

mantel scarf

Fabrics: "Thimbleberries Sunshine & Shadows" from RJR Fashion Fabrics.

As a tray liner and buffet roll-up, to hold eating utensils, and open as practical lap protection

1

2

3

4   back of napkin

5   napkin front

pocket

ribbon tie

Fabrics: "Bali Batiks" from Hoffman California International Fabrics. Appliqués: "Batik Chinese Proverb Blocks" from Island Batik, Inc.

As Coasters, Cozies & Covers

As a bottle coaster

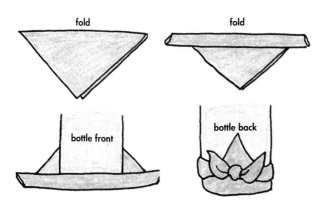

As a coffee press cozy or bottle wrap

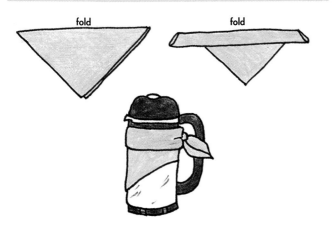

As a bottle cover

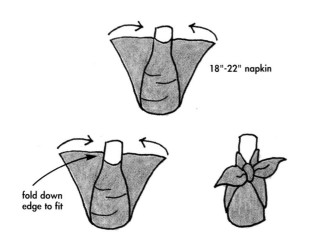

18"-22" napkin

fold down edge to fit

Ready-made napkins.

As a pitcher cover, to keep out insects and dust

Fabric: "Fall Medley" from Fabric Traditions.

As Pillows, Bolsters, Slipcovers & Table Toppers

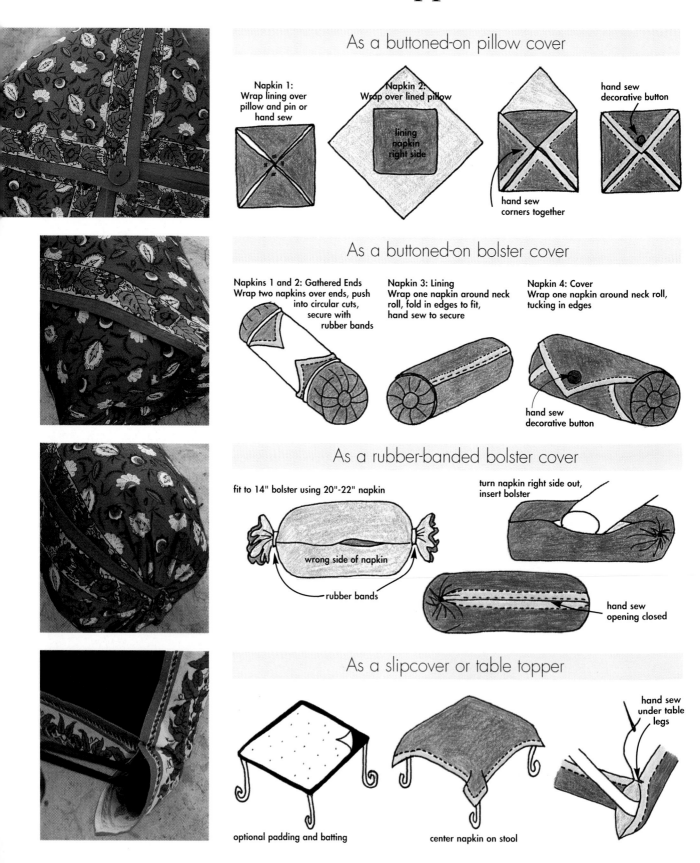

As a buttoned-on pillow cover

Napkin 1:
Wrap lining over pillow and pin or hand sew

Napkin 2:
Wrap over lined pillow

lining napkin right side

hand sew decorative button

hand sew corners together

As a buttoned-on bolster cover

Napkins 1 and 2: Gathered Ends
Wrap two napkins over ends, push into circular cuts, secure with rubber bands

Napkin 3: Lining
Wrap one napkin around neck roll, fold in edges to fit, hand sew to secure

Napkin 4: Cover
Wrap one napkin around neck roll, tucking in edges

hand sew decorative button

As a rubber-banded bolster cover

fit to 14" bolster using 20"-22" napkin

turn napkin right side out, insert bolster

wrong side of napkin

rubber bands

hand sew opening closed

As a slipcover or table topper

optional padding and batting

center napkin on stool

hand sew under table legs

As decorating squares, napkins make fast, affordable furnishings: pillows, bolsters, slipcovers, and table

toppers. Bordered napkins are favorites because the color-defined edges highlight hems and seams. Sewing

is minimal, so these napkins are readily converted for another use later – around the house or on the table.

As Décor

Vintage napkins from Mary's collection.

As a valance

Drape the napkins over the rod, as shown. If necessary, secure the layers together with double-stick tape. For longer rods on wider windows, add additional napkins, lapping them to fill the center section.

As a bulletin-board beautifier

Cover or accent an entire board, securing the napkins with double-stick tape or pins.

As Covers, Fillers & Accents

Tie the napkin on the throat of the vase, bandana style.

Same ready-made napkin used for all photos on this page.

Insert the napkin into the vase, distributing the ease. For a smaller top ruffle, fill the entire length of the vase, as shown on page 106.

As an accent for a vase (wet arrangement)

As a filler for a vase (dry arrangement)

As a cover for a vase (dry arrangement)

As a lampshade "slipcover"

Center the vase on the wrong side of the napkin and tuck the edges into the opening, distributing the ease.

Drape the napkin over the shade, determining the size of the centered top opening. Pink or serge the edge, then turn and edgestitch.*Optional:* Glue or sew on beaded trim.

As Aprons

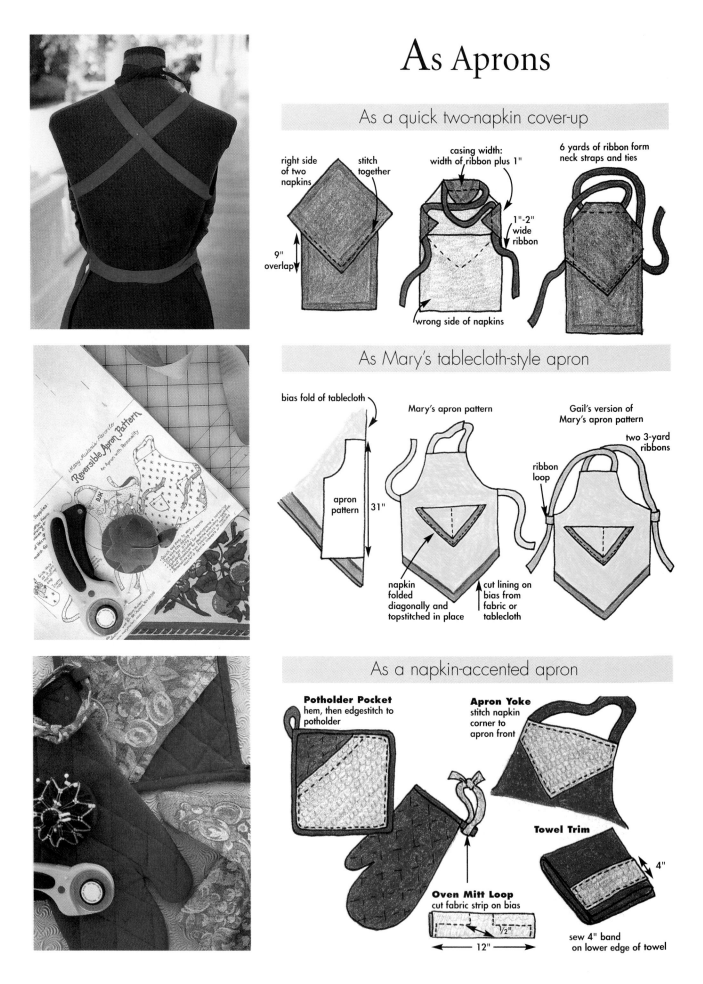

As a quick two-napkin cover-up

right side of two napkins

stitch together

9" overlap

casing width: width of ribbon plus 1"

1"-2" wide ribbon

wrong side of napkins

6 yards of ribbon form neck straps and ties

As Mary's tablecloth-style apron

bias fold of tablecloth

apron pattern

31"

Mary's apron pattern

napkin folded diagonally and topstitched in place

cut lining on bias from fabric or tablecloth

Gail's version of Mary's apron pattern

two 3-yard ribbons

ribbon loop

As a napkin-accented apron

Potholder Pocket
hem, then edgestitch to potholder

Apron Yoke
stitch napkin corner to apron front

Oven Mitt Loop
cut fabric strip on bias

1/2"

12"

Towel Trim

4"

sew 4" band on lower edge of towel

Aprons make great sense and napkins make great aprons. These stylish stain-preventers are perfect as gifts too – perhaps to give with a set of napkins? The durability of the aprons was tested on the way to this peaceful porch scene when Gail's dog Gunnar jumped into the back of her car – uninvited – on top of the mannequins.

As Totes

As a drawstring tote

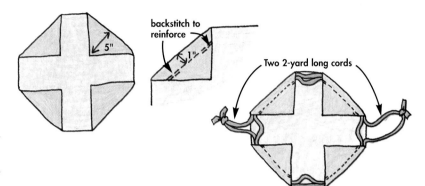

5"

backstitch to reinforce

1"

Two 2-yard long cords

As a two-napkin tote

two 18" x 1" webbing strips for handles

four 2" squares of Ultrasuede or nonfray fabric

sew squares over handle ends on two napkins

sew napkins together

As an easy envelope

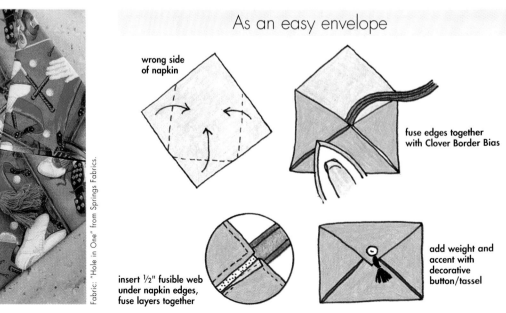

wrong side of napkin

fuse edges together with Clover Border Bias

insert ½" fusible web under napkin edges, fuse layers together

add weight and accent with decorative button/tassel

Chapter 9
Time- and Money-Saving Guide

Napkins from Mary's vintage collection. Tablecloth crocheted by her mother, Helmi Koski.

By choice or necessity, we all gravitate toward activities that are kind to our schedules and pocketbooks. With those realities clearly in mind, we have compiled our latest tips for napkin finishes, folds, and flourishes. "Yes, Virginia, there is space in your day – and budget – for these little squares of accessible elegance."

Be resourceful. Hand towels can double as lovely, practical napkins. When less presentable, retire them to the kitchen.

Napkin Fabrics: Key Questions & Sources

Fabric stores are filled with napkin-making possibilities. But we find materials – and ready-made napkins – through a wide range of sources.

Before buying napkin fabric – or ready-mades – ask these questions:

• **Is it washable and absorbent?** You can't go wrong with natural fibers like cotton or linen. Decorator fabric finishes diminish absorbency, but washing usually softens the surface adequately.

• **Is it wrinkle-prone?** This may or may not be a factor for you. Linen needs pressing, but looks beautiful on the table, and feels wonderful next to your skin. Polyester is definitely presentable, but if it's the only fiber in a fabric, it absorbs as well as plastic wrap. For the least pressing and the most absorbency, look for tightly woven cottons with some surface interest – quality batiks, for instance (see page 49).

• **Is there a definite right and wrong side?** If so, the wrong side may be revealed when the napkin is folded. Either add a lining layer or fold with another napkin as "lining" (see page 113).

• **Is the fabric heavy and firm enough to be used single layer?** Add a lining layer, or select another, heavier fabric.

• **Is there enough fabric to make multiples?** Refer to our yardages on page 117. If you're short of fabric, consider mixing prints and colors within the napkin set.

• **Is the fabric sized and firmly woven enough to hold three-dimensional or standing folds?** If not, choose other fabrics, or stick with softer folds.

• **Antique stores, thrift shops, estate sales, and auctions.** Dig through vintage linens and discarded yardage. Undamaged sections of curtains, tablecloths, slipcovers, sheets and dirndl skirts can be cut out as napkin fabric, too. (Also see Reviving Vintage Linens, page 114.)

• **Bedding departments.** Take advantage of white-sale bargains. Sheet dimensions can accommodate both napkins and a matching tablecloth.

• **Upholstery shops.** Seek out discounted remnants and sample sets. Wash after sewing, but before use, to increase absorbency.

• **Kitchen stores and catalogs.** You'll see trendy and surprisingly affordable napkins, often custom-coordinated to rings and dishes.

Upgrade inexpensive cotton bandanas by using double layers. Fuse the edges together and hem or serge-finish.

User-Friendly Folding Tips

"Line" with a second napkin. Or fold to create different looks with the same napkins.

What you won't need to master the folds featured in this book (pages 8 to 20): folding experience, lots of time, huge napkins, or extra pressing and starching. Have fun!

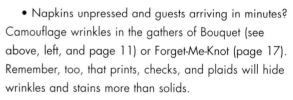

Fabric: "Bookbinders" from Timeless Treasures.

• Fold on any clean, flat surface. "Folding in the air" will prove to be an exercise in futility.

• Coordinate the napkin size, weight, and crispness to the fold you've chosen. Napkin guidelines are given with each fold illustrated in this book.

• If using hand towels, other rectangles, or any shape that isn't square, rolling works well (see pages 77, 78, and 112). *Optional*: Secure the roll-up with a ring or tie.

• "Line" an unlined or limp napkin by folding it with another napkin, either fabric or paper. To hide the wrong side of a single-sided print or solid, fold it with a lining layer, aligning the edges. Or add a border and weight by folding with a larger napkin, as shown on page 103.

• Need more crispness to stand up or pleat a napkin? Simply spray on starch and press. However, in keeping with our timesaving approach, none of the napkins in this book were starched before photography. You will notice our folded shapes are noticeably softer than those seen in catalogs and other napkin-folding books. Ours are less stiff and more absorbent when actually used, too. We like the look and the ease – and think you will, too.

• Napkins unpressed and guests arriving in minutes? Camouflage wrinkles in the gathers of Bouquet (see above, left, and page 11) or Forget-Me-Knot (page 17). Remember, too, that prints, checks, and plaids will hide wrinkles and stains more than solids.

• To maximize the size of a napkin, use a ring. For ring ideas, see pages 21 to 30.

• Fold to create different looks with the same napkins, as we've done with the napkins on this page (top, Bouquet, page 11, and lower, Flame, page 9).

• Store your napkins fold-ready: flat and unfolded. No drawer space? Drape them over a hanger and, if necessary, fasten them with clothespins or large safety pins. If the hanger creates unwanted creases, use an open-ended pant hanger instead. You can widen this type of hanger with a paper-towel or gift-wrap core, threaded on the bar.

• Fold with abandon. Encourage family and friends to join in the fun of inventing variations and original designs.

Reviving Vintage Linens

Are you storing – but never using – an inventory of heirloom linens? Or have you been tempted by collections sold at antique stores and auctions? Whether they are passed down from a family member or purchased, now is the time to use these vintage textile treasures, as is, or as embellishments.

Before and after Mary applied stain-removing techniques. Displayed on a tablecloth crocheted by her mother, Helmi Koski.

Stains and discoloration can be problems. Believe it or not, most can be solved without harsh chlorine bleach. Mary treated a set of stained vintage napkins (A), and was rewarded with bright, clean transformations (B) – without using chlorine bleach.

Try her safer and more effective steps to reviving vintage table linens:

1. Check the condition, color, and scent of the napkins first. If the piece is stained, yellowed, or dingy, our favorite way to prepare and renew old napkins is to soak them in water. That's right: Simply soak the napkins overnight or several hours. Soaking rehydrates and strengthens the fibers, allowing for more effective cleaning.

2. After soaking, remove the water and launder the napkins using a mild soap such as Ivory or Dreft. Set on a gentle washing machine cycle, or place the napkins in a mesh bag to reduce friction and agitation to the fibers.

3. Inspect the napkins after the first laundering. If they appear to be clean and unstained, dry and press them. We suggest drying on an outdoor clothesline. White napkins become even whiter when exposed to the sun. An indoor clothesline is the second choice.

4. If the napkins are still soiled, soak them again for several hours in water with oxygenated bleach such as OxyClean or detergent with washing soda added. Check the napkins periodically; remove them from soaking, and if necessary, launder them again. If an odor persists, soak the napkins in a mixture of water and white vinegar (about three to one ratio).

5. Continue to soak and launder in steps, reserving the harshest chemicals, such as chlorine bleach, for your final attempts to revive your vintage napkins.

Pressing: Keep the Spray Bottle Handy

Spray with water, and let them sit for an hour or two, allowing the wrinkles to loosen – just as your grandmother did. While pressing, continue to spray them with water to help flatten stubborn creases (some may never quite come out). Don't stress about these minor imperfections, which are all part of the charm and character of vintage natural fibers.

Optional: Apply spray-on starch for a crisper finish.

Rita Farro, our good friend, vintage-linen authority, and well-known public speaker, taught us all these tips. Check out her newest book, Dress Your Dream Bed, *another Krause publication.*

Serging: Gail's Tried & True Tips

Serging napkins is fast, almost sinful fun.
You can do it. Here's how.

Fabric: "Fall Medley" from Fabric Traditions.

• **Dust it off, take it out of the box or closet and/or plug it in.** Locate your manual – if possible. Breeze through routine maintenance, such as oiling and changing tired needles.

• **For napkin finishing, use Woolly Nylon (or any similar type of multifilament nylon thread) in all positions.** Why? First, the high-yardage cones let you serge for a long, long time without changing thread. Second, this soft multifilament thread is super strong and less inclined to pesky, time-consuming breakage. Third, Woolly Nylon stretches to enhance tension tightening, and spreads to cover the fabric edge. One more bonus: Woolly Nylon is nearly ravel-free, eliminating tying off and minimizing the need for seam sealant such as FrayBlock. *Caution:* Too-hot irons can melt Woolly Nylon, so press up to the stitching, or over a protective sheet or cloth.

• **Thread properly, following the prescribed paths for the needle and loopers.** Although the narrow *rolled* edge is synonymous with napkin edges (A in photo and page 82), I use narrow *balanced* serging for edges too stubborn to roll, as well as the wider wrapped stitch (B in photo and page 84) and basic balanced serging (see pages 80, 86, and 88). Check your manual or ask your dealer how to set up for these stitches.

• **Play with tensions on scrap fabric, similar in weight, weave, grain, and fiber to your napkins.** If you see too much thread, the tension needs tightening. If you see too little thread, or it is breaking, the thread needs to be loosened. Adjust one position at a time to better determine how that particular setting changes the stitch. If you change thread or fabric types, you will likely need to fine-tune some settings.

• **Note that stitch length and width adjustments also change tension.** As you widen or lengthen the stitch, the tensions will tighten. As you shorten or narrow the stitch, the tensions will loosen. The looper tensions will be changed the most dramatically with width and length adjustments, and the needle tension less so. Differential feed changes may also change the tension, so plan on some fine-tuning.

• **Stabilize napkin edges to guarantee serging success.** Using fusible web strips, fuse a lining layer to the napkin before serging (see page 82 and above). Or serge over water-soluble stabilizer to train the "hairy" fabric fibers under the narrow rolled edge.

• **If you're a beginner, or a bit rusty, stick with corners rather than curves.** It's much more difficult to serge a curve uniformly than it is to simply serge off the edge. Also, slightly rounded corners look squarer than skinny ones.

• **Never, ever, rip out serging on napkins.** Because precise size isn't crucial, simply re-serge the edge, trimming off the previous stitching. Even without adjustments, the second row will be more uniform because the first row stabilizes the edge.

• **Rely on basic serged finishing, turn and topstitch conventionally** (see page 80 and 88), if your narrow-rolled edges aren't narrow or rolled. Hemmed edges withstand rigorous use and laundering, too.

You'll find lots more serging solutions in the book *The Ultimate Serger Answer Guide: Troubleshooting for Any Overlock Brand or Model.*

Cutting Out: Our Timesaving Template System

For the fastest, most accurate cutting out, rely on this template system. Mary cuts her templates from poster board, then traces around the template and cuts the fabric with scissors. Gail uses utility shears to cut hers from a rotary mat, then rotary cuts around the template.

If you read nothing else in this book, read about the "template cutting system" described here. We've made dozens of napkins and have discovered that the #1 frustration, time, and accuracy saver was our cutting template method. Why? We'll explain – and try to convince you.

• **Ensure easy accuracy.** You will cut every napkin to a perfect square, no matter what the grain imperfections or how tired you are.

• **Instantly determine if there's enough fabric** for one, or multiples of a napkin. There's little or no measuring required and no pinning whatsoever. (Somehow a pincushion found its way into our photo – sorry for the cute but confusing prop.)

• **Safeguard your fabric** by eliminating grain pulls from tearing, or waste from inaccurate cutting.

• **Work in tandem with either scissors** or our tools of choice: cutting mats and rotary cutters.

• **Quickly mark** for other creative grain possibilities, such as bias napkins (see pages 56 and 86).

Note: *Both of us are sold on this system, and plan to expand our template inventories to include 19", 21", and 23" sizes.*

Mary's Poster Board Templates

Mary began with three templates cut from standard poster board: squares of 18", 20", and 22". She immediately saw how easy it was to cut napkins from fabric with the template guides lined up parallel to the selvage edges. (To prevent puckering, Mary trims off the selvage edges.) After securing the boards with weights, she traces around the templates with a chalk marker or a pen, then cuts out the fabric with scissors.

Gail's Cutting Mat Templates

Gail liked the template idea and made hers from rotary cutting mats. She used a pair of utility shears to carefully cut the mat to the template size. (She did admit to slightly sore hands.) Then she could quickly cut out napkins with a rotary cutter around the template on top of a larger rotary cutting mat.

Napkin Sizes: Our Unsolicited and Opinionated Advice

In our experiences of using and making napkins, we have developed preferences for sizes and fabrics. For a dinner napkin, we like 20" to 22" sizes, especially if the fabric is a single layer. If the napkin is lined, an 18" napkin is acceptable because it is more substantial. Believe it or not, fabric quality comes into play, too – crummy fabrics look smaller and perform in a diminished fashion. So look for fabrics that will age well, through the abuse of meals, washing, and drying. Your time is worthy of better materials.

Here's a handy chart to help you shop for napkin fabrics. The napkin sizes are listed with their square measurements before hemming. Photocopy (reduce and/or laminate as desired) and keep it in your wallet for reference when fabric shopping.

Simply Napkins' Handy Napkin Size and Yardage Chart

Sizes indicated are unfinished. Yardages are calculated for 44"/45" wide fabric.

Square Napkin Size	Yardage for Four Napkins	Binding or Trim for Four Napkins
6" coaster size	⅙ yard	2¾ yards
10" cocktail size	⅓ yard	5 yards
15" lunch or tea size	⅚ yard	7 yards
18" lunch or dinner	1 yard	8¼ yards
20" dinner	1⅛ yards	9¼ yards
22" dinner	1¼ yards	10 yards

More Creative Cutting Out

Rounding Corners: Use a cup or tool like the Radial Rule.

Round Napkins: Cut a square first, then quarter fold neatly. Use a template or measuring tape to mark the radius. After cutting out, refold to check for symmetry. If you are going to cut out lots of round napkins, we recommend first making a template from poster board.

Note: *Cornerless round napkins can look skimpy if they are smaller than 18" in diameter, finished. Our preference? No smaller than 20" finished diameter.*

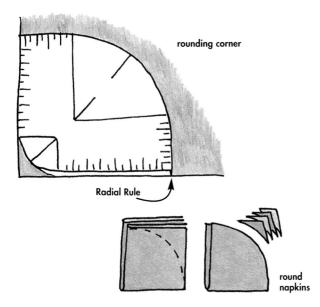

rounding corner

Radial Rule

round napkins

Bias Napkins: Simply turn the template so the edge forms a 45° angle with the lengthwise or crosswise grain.

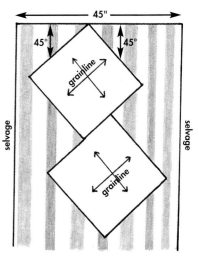

45"

45°   45°

selvage   grainline   grainline   selvage

Bias Strips: Yardages & How-Tos

Fabric: "Bird Tree" from Springs Quilters Only Fabrics. Binding: Clover Border Bias.

Whether you buy it or make your own, bias tape offers great options for napkin creations. Purchased bias tape saves cutting and sewing time, whereas making your own is more affordable and less limiting in color and width options.

One 2½ yard package of bias tape is adequate for binding one 18", 20", or 22" napkin. One 6½ yard roll of fusible Clover Border Bias (½" width, as shown in the photo above and on page 50) will cover the edges of three 18" napkins or two 20" or 22" napkins. One 11 yard roll of Clover Quick Bias (⅛" or ¼" widths) will trim all the edges of four 18" or 20" napkins.

As we mentioned before, there are trade-offs when comparing purchased and ready-made binding. Advantages of making your own bias tape include selecting any fabric print or solid and creating a continuous length of tape for numerous napkins. The fabric square generally costs less than purchased bias tape, but more sewing and pressing time is required.

To make bias tape, begin with a square of fabric cut to the size listed in the chart on page 119.

Note: *Because Gail stockpiles way too much fabric, she prefers fewer piecing seams, so generally uses twice as much yardage as indicated on our chart. It's up to you!*

Easy Steps for Making Bias Tape

1. Cut a fabric square (see chart on page 119). Draw a diagonal line on the square and cut on the line to create two triangles.

2. With the right sides of the fabric together, match edges (A) and (B). Straight stitch them together using a ¼" seam allowance and a short stitch length. (Strong seams are important.) Press the seam open.

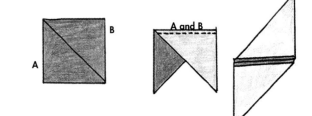

3. Mark the width of the bias strip (cut 1 1/2" wide for a finished 1/2" bias or 3/4" wide for a finished 1/4" bias) and cut in to the edge about 2". Mark a dot on the opposite edge of the fabric.

4. Bring the cut edge to the dot and pin the edges together. Sew a 1/4" seam allowance and press the seam open. The fabric piece is now a tube.

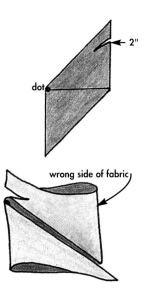

wrong side of fabric

5. Measure, mark, and cut the tube to create a continuous strip of bias. For 1/4" bias, trim the seam allowances and corners to remove bulk.

6. Turn under and press the edges of the bias or pull the tape through a Clover Bias Tape Maker and press. To make 1/2" wide tape to wrap the napkin edges, fold and lightly press the bias strip in half. **Note:** *For a slightly narrower 3/8" wide finished tape, fold the 1 1/2" wide strip edges in so they meet in the center.*

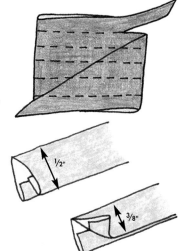

Bias Binding Strips: Yardage Yields from Squares

1/2" Bias for Four Edges (strip width 1 1/2")		1/4" Trim on One Edge (strip width 3/4")	1/4" Trim for Four Edges (strip width 3/4")
(4) 18" napkins	23" square	9" square	16" square
(4) 20" napkins	24" square	10" square	17" square

Bonus: Back-to-Front Binding

Back-to-front binding has become one of our most reliable edge-finishing methods (see Foundation Strips, Fast, page 70 and Quick "Snowball" Corners, page 72). It's really not a binding at all, but the lining wrapped over the top of the napkin.

Fold two opposite napkin edges over 3/8" twice to the top side of the napkin. Straight stitch in place, close to the inside folded edge of the binding. Repeat for the remaining two edges. *Optional:* Fold to miter the corners as shown. (A)

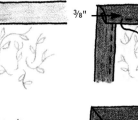

Hemstitching: A Classic Returns

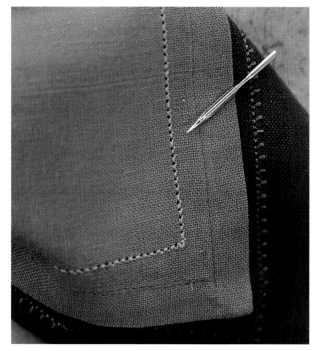

Re-create the look of hemstitching by using a "wing" sewing machine needle.

Hemstitching, long a tradition in table linens, is now being seen on the trendiest ready-mades. Add this subtly stylish detail to your napkins, sewn or purchased, by simply using a "wing" sewing machine needle.

Embroidery design: "Design 7, Christmas II 1014" from Janome.

Work hemstitching along (above) or parallel to (left) the hemline stitching.

- **Select napkins or fabrics that are medium to densely woven and heavier weight.** (Linens and linen blends work well.)

- **Apply Perfect Sew Liquid Stabilizer** or two to three applications of spray starch to stiffen the fabric. Use the stitching line on a completed napkin as a guide and sew a presser foot width from that line.

- **Purchase a wing needle** – size 100 is suitable for most napkins. Test on a fabric scrap, experimenting with a variety of stitches. Machine stitches that move back and forth through the same needle holes form larger openings for more dramatic hemstitched looks. The stitch we found closest to hemstitching is a repetitive straight stitch, shown in the photo, along with the repetitive blanket stitch. **Note**: *Real hemstitching is worked with a hemstitching machine.*

- **Select a thread color to blend closely with the napkin color**, or slightly lighter or darker for a bit more visibility. For clarity, a higher contrast thread was used for our samples here.

- **Begin stitching along the napkin edge** rather than in the corner. Be daring and avoid sewing boredom – try a different stitch in each quarter of the napkin!

- **Soak the napkins in clear water** after you've completed the stitching to remove the starch or stabilizing treatments.

Hemstitching often appears along the edges of vintage linens, such as Mary's heirloom napkins.

Easiest Machine Embroidery Strategies

After viewing Chapter 7: Machine Embroidery Showcase, you are sure to be inspired to try your hand at embroidering napkins yourself. For less stress and more creative serenity, try these strategies.

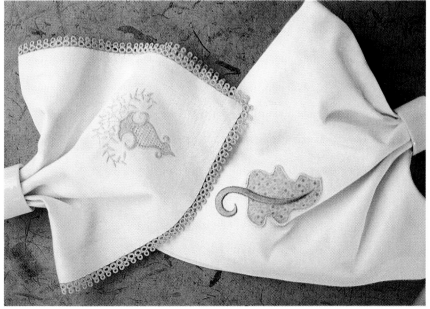

Embroidery designs: "WN Sconce" from the Criswelll Lace Wing Collection and Mary Mulari's leaf appliqué from Amazing Designs card #3005.

• **Don't waste your time or materials embroidering on crummy fabrics or napkins.**

• **Take time to carefully select a design**, from simple to intricate. Remember that the design will be stitched many times, once on each napkin you decorate. You may not enjoy the project after changing the thread color four or five times on eight napkins (we know this to be true!). A simple design with one or two thread color changes and a low stitch count, or a single letter monogram, are all safe choices for those short on time or expertise. Also consider reducing the size of the design within the 4" x 4" hoop.

• **Test stitch the design** you've chosen, using a piece of fabric hemmed as a napkin would be. Most embroidery experts recommend hooping only the stabilizer and holding the napkin corner in place with temporary spray fusible such as Sulky KK2000. Suggested stabilizers include tear-away varieties such as Sulky Tear-Easy, Finishing Touch Ultra Tear Away, OESD Ultra Clean and Tear, Pellon Tear-N-Wash, and water-soluble varieties such as OESD Badgemaster, Aqua Magic, and Sulky Super Solvy. If one layer of tear-away stabilizer is not stable enough in embroidery practice, use two layers.

• **Use the test stitching or a photocopy of the test stitching to help determine the center of the design** and also the placement of the design on the napkins. Avoid the hem of the napkin when placing the design.

• **Fold and press the practice fabric and the napkins diagonally at the corner.** Then fold and press a line across the diagonal fold to mark the center of the design. Spray the back of the practice fabric with temporary spray fusible such as Sulky KK2000 and finger press it in place on the hooped stabilizer. For guidelines to help in positioning the fabric, place the hoop with stabilizer on a gridded table or rotary cutting mat. Line up the pressed perpendicular lines with the center horizontal and vertical lines on the embroidery hoop.

• **Choose bobbin thread to match either the top thread color or the napkin color.** After the stitching is complete, remove the stabilizer and the practice fabric from the hoop. Check the design size, position, and thread color choices and make adjustments before stitching on the napkins. Record any changes in the design before turning off the machine, in case you don't complete your embroidery in one sewing session.

• **Consider stitching a different design on each napkin corner.** The variety of designs will be a conversation starter at your dinner table.

Our sincere thanks to the many companies, and their embroidery specialists, who contributed designs to this book (pages 89 to 96). Take a trip to your local sewing machine dealer soon to see the latest in today's wonderful stitching technology.

Mary's Monograms

Personalize napkins with initials – one or a combination. We've included two sizes of the same alphabet for first and last name initials, as shown. The alphabets are printed backwards for ease in tracing on paper-backed fusible web. After the letters are traced, fused, and cut out of fabric, they'll be facing in the right direction for your napkins.

For stitching the monograms in place, refer to the instructions for appliqué on page 124. For the easiest cutting out and stitching, start with a ravel-free fabric such as Ultrasuede or Sensuede.

Fabrics: Ultrasuede from Toray and "Bird Tree" from Springs Quilters Only Fabrics.

Find the pattern for this Nifty Napkin Cone on page 27. Flip the monogram if you want the pointed side toward you.

Appliqué fabric: "Bali Batik" from Hoffman California International Fabrics on ready-made napkin.

Monogram appliqués on a ready-made napkin.

Use larger letters for the last name initial and smaller letters for the first or first and middle names.

Mary's Appliqués: Tips & Designs

• **If necessary, reduce or enlarge your appliqué choice**. Then trace a design on paper-backed fusible web (Therm O Web HeatnBond Lite or Pellon Wonder Under). Fuse it to the wrong side of the appliqué fabric. Cut out the design and peel off the paper backing.

• **Position the appliqué on the napkin and fuse it in place**. Pin tear-away stabilizer on the wrong side of the napkin, under the appliqué.

• **Stitch around the appliqué** with a medium width satin stitch (a zigzag stitch adjusted to 2.5 width and .5 or .3 length). Test the stitch on scraps first. (Gail prefers faster stitching and less thread density, so she often uses a longer stitch or even a straight stitch.) Pull the top threads to the wrong side of the napkin and trim. Remove the stabilizer from the back of the napkin.

Ready Reference: Table Setting Templates

We photocopied and laminated this page of table setting templates and suggest that you do the same. Then, for quick reference, keep it in a handy drawer or tape it to the inside of a cabinet. (Gail reminds her family to study the setting – and puts them to work.) Remember, however, that these are just table setting guides, not laws. Feel free to devise your own table setting schemes, altering elements and placements. *Our only dictate: Enjoy each other, and your meal.*

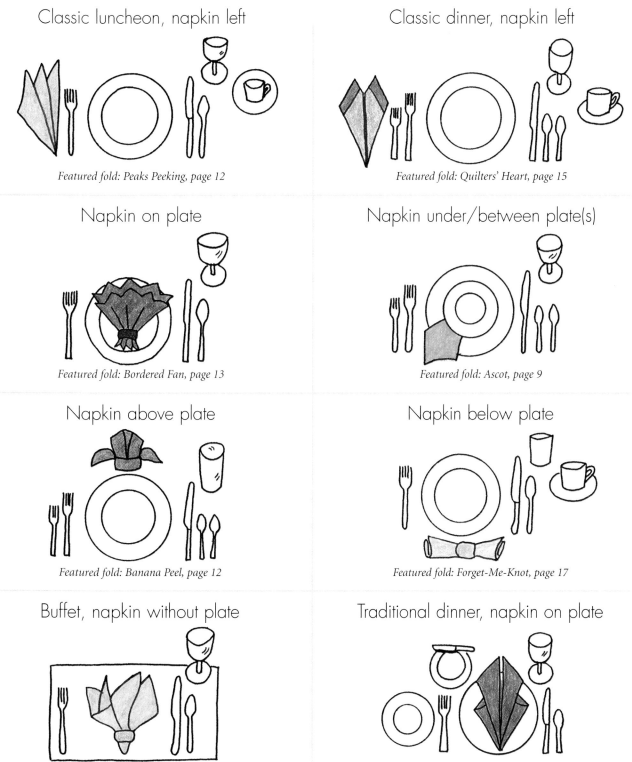

Classic luncheon, napkin left
Featured fold: Peaks Peeking, page 12

Classic dinner, napkin left
Featured fold: Quilters' Heart, page 15

Napkin on plate
Featured fold: Bordered Fan, page 13

Napkin under/between plate(s)
Featured fold: Ascot, page 9

Napkin above plate
Featured fold: Banana Peel, page 12

Napkin below plate
Featured fold: Forget-Me-Knot, page 17

Buffet, napkin without plate
Featured fold: Bouquet, page 11

Traditional dinner, napkin on plate
Featured fold: Rolled Flair, page 13

About the Authors

Mary Mulari is an author and much sought-after public speaker and teacher. Despite her busy production and traveling schedules, she has written 17 books including *Made for Travel* and *Denim & Chambray with Style*. Mary displays her practical know-how and subtle Midwestern wit as a guest on *Sewing with Nancy* and *America Sews with Sue Hausmann* (both PBS TV) and as a seminar presenter. Also a popular artist, she designs for Amazing Designs (machine embroidery) and Marcus Brothers Textiles, as well as for her own pattern line. Mary lives, works, skis, kayaks and collects vintage linens in Aurora, Minnesota, but stays connected with readers, audiences and fans worldwide through her steadily growing body of work and her Web site (marymulari.com).

For 30 years, **Gail Brown** has been writing about how to sew, serge, and decorate better – and faster. *Simply Napkins* is her 14th title. Her books include one of the industry's all-time bestsellers, *The Ultimate Serger Answer Guide*. She is internationally recognized for her many television and video appearances on *Sewing with Nancy* (PBS), *Sew Perfect* (HGTV), and *Our Home* (Viacom/Lifetime).

Napkins are her sewing project – and gift – of choice. From Gail's home office in Hoquiam, Washington, she plays with all things digital, designs head covers for hair-loss sufferers, and generally doesn't let reality get in the way. She continues to write for *Sew News* ("From the Heart"), the *Creative Kindness* Web site (creativekindness.com), and her own Web site (gailbrown.com).

Mary Mulari and Gail Brown

Sources for Napkin Making (and Napkins)

Simply Napkins simply wouldn't have happened without the generous assistance, in know-how and products, from many companies. Look for their products in fabric stores and departments, sewing machine dealerships, through mail order, and on the Internet. Find additional sources listed in sewing, embroidery, quilting, and crafting magazines.

Sewing Machine Companies

Find your local dealer on these Web sites, as well as product information.

Babylock USA
babylock.com

Bernina of America
berninausa.com

Brother International
brother.com
brothermall.com

Elna USA
elnausa.com

Janome America
janome.com

Kenmore
Sears.com

Pfaff American Sales Corp.
pfaffusa.com

Simplicity
simplicitysewing.com

Singer Company
singerco.com

Viking Sewing Machines
husqvarnaviking.com

White
whitesewing.com

Embroidery Design Companies

Amazing Designs
amazingdesigns.com

Cactus Punch
cactuspunch.com

Criswell Embroidery and Design
k-lace.com

Dakota Collectibles
dakotacollectibles.com

Embroidery Arts
embroideryarts.com

Martha Pullen Co.
marthapullen.com

Oklahoma Embroidery Supply & Design (OESD)
embroideryonline.com

Sudberry House
sudberry.com

Suzanne Hinshaw
suzannehnshaw.com

Vermillion Stitchery
vsccs.com

Mail Order Notions

Clotilde
(800) 772-2891
clotilde.com
Notions, books, machines

Diane Ericson
revisions-ericson.com
Patterns and stencils

Home-Sew
(800) 344-4739
homesew.com
Trims, bindings, findings

June Tailor
junetailor.com
Inkjet transfer fabric, décor forms

Keepsake Quilting
keepsakequilting.com
Fabrics, tools, patterns

Mary's Productions
Box 87-SNS
Aurora, MN 55705
(218) 229-2804
marymulari.com
Books, fabrics, seminars

Nancy's Notions
(800) 833-0690
nancysnotions.com
Notions, books, fabrics, machines

See-Thru Stamps
purrfection.com
Stamping supplies

Fabric Companies

Note: *These companies sell through retailers, not directly to consumers.*

Concord House
concordhouse.com

Dan River Inc.
danriver.com

Fabric Traditions
fabrictraditions.com

FreeSpirit Fabrics
freespiritfabric.com

Hoffman California International Fabrics
hoffmanfabrics.com

Marcus Brothers Textiles
marcusbrothers.com

Michael Miller Fabrics
michaelmillerfabrics.com

P & B Textiles
PBtex.com

RJR Fashion Fabrics
RJRFabrics.com

Spring Creative Products Group
springs.com

Timeless Treasures Fabrics
TTfabrics.com

VIP by Cranston
vipbycranston.com

Ready-Made Napkins

Crate and Barrel
crateandbarrel.com

JC Penney
jcpenney.com

Kitchen Links
kitchenlinks.net
Also dishes, accessories

Pottery Barn
potterybarn.com

Sur La Table
surlatable.com

Williams and Sonoma
williams-sonoma.com

Note: *Special thanks to the following for the fun dishes and props: Harbor Drug & Gifts and Peoples Emporium Antiques, both of Hoquiam, Washington, and the Grand Heron, Kitchen Links, and The Jitterbug, all of Aberdeen, Washington.*

Index

appliqué, 3, 39, 40, 89, 80-81, 22-124
apron, 108-109
banner napkin, 78
basket fillers, liners, accents, 100
Beautiful Borders, 62-63
bias,
    borders, 76-77
    strips, buying and making, 118-119
binding, 50-51, 70-73, 86-87, 119
blooming napkins, 99, 100
bolsters, napkins as covers, 97, 104-105
border prints, 44-45, 104-105
buffet roll-up, 100, 102
bulletin board cover/accent, 106
Buttonhole Corner Napkin, 66
care,
    of napkins, 113
    of vintage napkins and linens, 114
Chopsticks Pockets, and Appliqués, 40
cones, napkin, 27, 122
cording, 64-65
Clever Corded Wonder, 64-65
Clover Border Bias, 50-51, 68-69, 118
Corner Danglers & Dazzlers, 38
Custom Color Copier Creations, 39
Cutting Out: Our Timesaving Template System, 116-117
décor, napkins as, 100-107
Double-Needle Delights, 60-61
embroidery design companies, 89-96, 127
fabric companies, 127
fabrics, selection and care, 112
Fail-Proof Fused & Stitched Binding, 50-51
Fantastically Fast-Fused, 42-43
Fast, Fabulous Folds, 7-21
Fast-Framed Finish, 48-49
Fat Quarter Banner Napkins, 78-79
Fat Quarter Collection: Bias-Taped Borders, 68
folding tips, 113
folds, 7-20
Foundation Strips, Fast, 70-71
Four-Way Diagonal Napkins, 74
fused edges, 42-43
fusible transfer web, 42-43, 110
gift wrap, 99
gift sets, 98
Gorgeous Garnishes: Stamping, 32-33
hemstitching, 120
Hemstitching: A Classic Returns, 120
Holiday Folds: Table Top Trees, 20
jam prevention, 64

Koski, Helmi, 111, 114
Lapped-Trim Finish, 88
Lined and Reversible, 54-55
Lined, Fast-Fused Napkins, 52
lined napkins, 44-51, 54-55, 62-63, 70-75, 80-85
machine embroidery, 121
Machine Embroidery Showcase, 89-96
Machine-Sewn in Minutes, 53-66
mail-order sources, 127
marking and cutting out, 116-117
Mary's Monograms, 122-123
Mary's Simple Stenciling—With Style, 34-35
miters, folded, 80, 88
miters, stitched, 56-57
monogrammed napkins, 122-124
More Fat Quarter Bounty: Bias Borders, 76-77
Mulari, Mary, 6, 126
Napkins as Gifts and Décor, 97-110
napkin
    cones, 27, 122
    rings, 21-30
    supplies and sources, 127
Narrow-Rolled Edges, 82-83
Narrow Serged and Turned, 88-89
needles,
    twin (double), 60-61
    wing, 120
no-sew techniques, 32-37, 42-43
pillows, napkins as covers, 97, 104-105
Place Card Windows, 40
placemats, napkins as, 47, 102
pressing napkins, 112-113
Quick Fuse Inkjet Fabric, 31, 39, 70
Quick "Snowball" Corners, 72-73
Quilt Lovers' Napkins, 67-76

quilting techniques for napkins, 67-78
ready-made napkins, sources for, 127
rick-rack, as napkin trim, 52, 82-83
Round, Fast-Fused Napkins, 52
round napkins, 52, 117
Rings: Ease, Elegance...Extraordinary! 21-30
runner, napkins as, 102
serging techniques, 79-87
Serging: Gail's Tried & True Tips, 115
sewing machine companies, 89-96, 127
setting a table using napkins, 125
Silk Floral Accents, 36-37
special occasion settings, 101
stamping, 32-33
stenciling, 34-35
Stitched-On Bound Edge, 78
storing napkins, 113
Table Setting Templates, 125
template system for cutting out napkins, 116-117
Terrific Topstitched Tubes, 46-47
totes, napkins as, 110
transferring images to fabric, 31, 39, 70
Trimmed Edges, 66
Twice-Turned Hems, 58-59
twin (double) needles, 60-61
Two-Seams: Simple Self-Lining, 44-45
valance, napkins as, 106
vase covers, fillers and accents, 107
vintage linens, reviving and care, 114
wing needles, 120
Woolly Nylon, 82-83, 84-85
wrapped corners, 54
Wrapped-Edge Finish, 84-85
yardage chart for napkins, 117
Zieman, Nancy, 6, 67, 77, 126

Not just for people and dogs: Gail's 27-pound cat, Big Kitty Quigg, looks natty in his napkin neck scarf.